James Thompson

Applied Theatre

Bewilderment and Beyond

PETER LANG

Oxford • Bern • Berlin • Bruxelles • Frankfurt/M. • New York • Wien

Bibliographic information published by Die Deutsche Bibliothek
Die Deutsche Bibliothek lists this publication in the Deutsche National-
bibliografie; detailed bibliographic data is available on the Internet at
‹http://dnb.ddb.de›.

British Library and Library of Congress Cataloguing-in-Publication Data:
A catalogue record for this book is available from *The British Library*,
Great Britain, and from *The Library of Congress*, USA

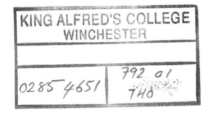
ISSN 1660-2560
ISBN 3-03910-021-1
US-ISBN 0-8204-6290-X

© Peter Lang AG, European Academic Publishers, Bern 2003
Hochfeldstrasse 32, Postfach 746, CH-3000 Bern 9, Switzerland
info@peterlang.com, www.peterlang.com, www.peterlang.net

Printed in Germany

To Debbie, with love

The act is beautiful if it provokes,
and leads us in our throats to discover, song

Jean Genet

This life is more than just a read thru

Red Hot Chilli Peppers

Contents

Acknowledgements

The research for this book was completed while on a Leverhulme Special Research Fellowship. I would like to thank the Leverhulme Trust for this opportunity and for the dedicated research time that it gave me. Without the support of the Trust, this book would not have been completed.

This book is a product of many discussions, meetings and projects. Many different people have inspired it in different ways. The first thanks should go to Paul Heritage, who provided invaluable comments on an early draft and offered honest and vital criticism. My debt to Paul lies also in the fact that many of the projects that appear in these pages were done with him or directed by him. We both know that we could not have visited Burkina alone. Additional thanks are due to all the people who work with Paul at People's Palace Projects and the School of English and Drama at Queen Mary, University of London – Catrin John, Caoimhe McAvinchey, Lois Weaver, Ali Campbell, Rose Sharp and Sarah Hussain.

Manchester University Drama Department colleagues deserve special thanks for the tolerance they have shown to my frequent absences from the country. Major thanks especially to Viv Gardner, who has been massively supportive and encouraged all aspects of applied theatre work in the department. All the colleagues in the Centre for Applied Theatre Research have helped to develop the ideas behind this book: particular thanks to Jenny Hughes who read early drafts and kept me on my political toes. Also, thank you to Julie McCarthy for commenting on my single-mindedness! Final thanks to Ken Richards for advice and comments on a near-final draft.

The book has been completed around numerous visits to run workshops and learn from projects in Sri Lanka. The people of the Big Circle network are an inspiration to anybody interested in applied theatre, and discussions with them have been invaluable in developing ideas. Thank you to you all. A particular thanks to Irene Fraser, whose dedication to facilitating applied theatre, as well as a chance meeting on a beach, has made much of this work possible.

Many of the projects commented on in the book were developed while I worked for the TIPP Centre. This organisation continues to work tirelessly and is an exceptional example of applied theatre practice. Thanks particularly to Simon Ruding and Kate McCoy, who continue to dedicate themselves to theatre in criminal justice settings.

All the students past and present on the Applied Theatre MA course in the Drama Department have in their own ways contributed to the ideas offered here. Discussions, debates and arguments with these groups have played a significant part in developing my thinking on this field, and they need to be acknowledged as the invisible contributors to this book. Many of these people are now working on applied-theatre projects and are developing the practice in many innovative and exciting directions.

Parts of the introduction and one chapter have appeared in earlier forms in various journals. I would like to thank the editors and publishers for the rights to reproduce this work. They are the *Applied Theatre Researcher*, *Community, Work and Family* and *The Annual Review of Critical Psychology*.

My final thanks go to Debbie, Hannah and Leah. No writing can ever be completed without a wonderful reason for pausing and having to talk, listen and play. Hannah and Leah – you are stars – yes means no and no means yes!

Applied Theatre

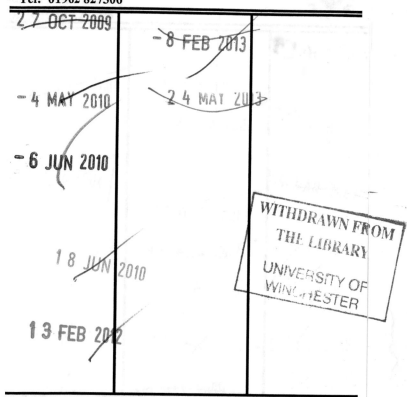

S T S S
STAGE and SCREEN STUDIES

Volume 5

Edited by
Kenneth Richards

PETER LANG
Oxford • Bern • Berlin • Bruxelles • Frankfurt/M. • New York • Wien

Preface
'Applied', a preface to 'theatre'

'Applied theatre' has become an increasingly popular term, used by
theatre practitioners from a diverse range of settings and countries to
categorise or explain their work. It has emerged in response to practice
in a number of different social policy or educational contexts and it is
grounded in a history of theatre that has sought to operate beyond the
boundaries of theatre buildings. Here in the UK it is also a product of
the practicalities of creating an engaged, participatory theatre in the
particularly brutal and unforgiving economic environment of the
1980s and 1990s. Applied theatre developed under the combined
effect of a harsh funding climate and the post-cold-war impact of
postmodernism. A desire to take 'theatre to the people' was divided
into creating theatre with a multitude of peoples (prisoners, disabled
groups, the elderly, children and so forth) and idealism was tempered
with a pragmatic search for sites where theatre practice could gain
non-arts financial support. In 2002, alongside the involvement of
companies and individuals, applied theatre has also become firmly
established inside the higher-education sector, with the term appearing
in the titles of undergraduate and postgraduate courses, centres for
research in the UK and Australia and modules in universities from
North America to Sri Lanka. It is therefore practised, taught and
researched without, I would argue, commensurate attention being
given to understanding its meaning. This book is therefore part of a
necessary debate about what it has been, what it is and what it could
be. Each chapter uses areas of theatre application – predominantly
prisons and development settings – to explore problems and possibilities for the 'field'. The book does not aim to be a conclusive text.
Instead, it offers a particular approach to applied theatre through a
series of chapters that individually cover very different issues.
Through these discussions, the book offers a way of seeing the work
that I hope will be questioned and challenged by alternative accounts.

One of the purposes of this preface, however, is to explain how I will be using the term and to outline some of the problems in its use. Applied theatre can cast a wide net, and it is important to examine some of the practices that are pulled in during that process. The metaphor of the net is deliberate, in that applied theatre brings together related fields as much as it constitutes its own. It is a collective and collecting term whose use has emerged before a strict definition has been agreed. For example, it has been welcomed by many who do not like the strict line that is often drawn between 'third world' 'theatre for development' and 'first world' 'community theatre'. The term 'applied theatre' insists that theatre in the marginal, excluded and impoverished areas of the UK has much to learn from theatre created in, for example, Burkina Faso in West Africa. Similarly in teaching, it has supported a sharing of knowledge drawn from the fields of theatre in education, drama in education, and theatre for social change. In practice it has meant the experiences of theatre in specific communities – for example with prisoners, with disabled people or with the elderly – are brought into dialogue with each other. It is a term that joins different categories of a socially engaged theatre without denying their separate histories or dictating what can be placed within their own boundaries. It seems, for example, to claim community-based participatory theatre, but is more equivocal about dramatherapy or psychodrama. These tendencies are often as arbitrary as they are well considered. This book does not seek to offer a final definition of the term, but instead argues that it is a useful phrase for a theatre that claims usefulness. It is imperfect. It is a term cast in different places, and therefore it will catch different practices according to the theatre histories of the places from which it is thrown. Operating in Brazil it will engage different traditions to those in the UK. This book considers practices that are particular to my experience and makes no claims that they are definitive.

The problem, of course, with a term that collects other practices, is that it can be accused of both denying differences and also seeking to claim a range of projects that do not wish to be included in its all-consuming reach. It is important, therefore, to acknowledge where the specifics or particularities of applied theatre are, as well as where it is a more general or boundaryless term. We need to consider where its definition is rightly fluid and where it should become fixed. The debate between the open and the fixed is repeated and reformulated in different guises throughout this book. It appears in the use of the term 'bewilderment' (see below), in a discussion of ethics, in questioning the notion of orthodoxy and around principles of practice. One place to start this discussion however is by noting that the two words in 'applied theatre' hide others. There are referents in the term that are not made explicit. For example, an object is hinted at – a place, person, community, issue or 'thing' to which theatre is applied. I would argue that it is because these 'things' are unspecified, that the discussions between various practices become possible. Theatre in education talks to theatre in prisons. In addition, the term conceals its subject. The person, group or community doing the applying is invisible and this allows theatre *by* elderly people to come into dialogue with theatre *for* youth. The debate focuses upon the verb, the action of application, and not the specifics of the agent or the place. Because it is based on that action, it permits the zones to be different and the types of theatre to be varied. Applied theatre becomes a practice that engages with the politics of prepositions. The theatres 'of', 'by', 'with' or 'for' question each other because none is given primacy in the term. These unspoken elements stimulate the debate between the different practices. Unquestioningly claiming 'theatre in education', 'prison theatre' or 'theatre for development' as part of a wider 'applied theatre' field should be rejected. However, the term is welcomed in the first instance for the discussions that it permits.

While noting the unspecified, it is also important to write about applied theatre's visible components. As I mention above, there are 'specifics' or given features of applied theatre. These need to be acknowledged and in my definition include the following. *Applied theatre* projects always take place in communities, in institutions or with specific groups. They often include the practice of theatre where it is least expected; for example, in prisons, refugee camps, forgotten estates, hospitals, museums, centres for the disabled, old people's homes and under-served rural villages: sometimes in theatres. Applied theatre is a participatory theatre created by people who would not usually make theatre. It is, I would hope, a practice by, with and for the excluded and marginalised. It is, at its best, a theatre that translates and adapts to the unfamiliar. It is a theatre wedded to vital issues and one that values debate. In circumstances where fear is dominant, it can be a theatre of celebration. In circumstances where celebratory escapism is dominant, it can be the theatre of serious enquiry. It should aim to be a theatre that somehow balances the pragmatism involved in making itself relevant in difficult environments with the idealism of a belief in transformation. Applied-theatre programmes can be a vital part of the way that people engage in their communities, reflect on issues and debate change. They can be central to different groups' experience of making and remaking their lives

The theatre that is made is neither simple nor singular in form. It can be the rough improvised naturalism of a prison theatre group and the well-crafted, dance-filled performance of a youth theatre. It could include HIV/AIDS education Forum theatre or Shakespeare in a secure hospital (Cox, 1992). The majority of the theatre forms discussed within this book are in some way derived from the 'theatre of the oppressed' tradition of Augusto Boal. This is exhibited in the centrality offered to participatory workshops, the blurring of spectator and audience divisions and the role of interactive 'forum'-style performances. Boal, I would contend, offers a powerful model of practice that is adaptable to a range of communities in diverse situations. The applicability and flexibility of the arsenal of techniques in the 'theatre of the oppressed' (Boal, 1992) is evidenced in their widespread use in Europe, the Americas, parts of Africa and Asia. However, it must be acknowledged that the focus on Boal is also arbitrary. It is a product of a UK environment where extended exposure to his writings and workshops over the last twenty years has made many applied and community-based theatre practitioners, including myself, take inspiration from his techniques. Boal thus has a strong place in this book out of a considered choice and importantly as a result of this specific history. His dominant position in the writing here should not be taken as an indication or an assertion that applied theatre must only take formal inspiration from one source. All applied-theatre practitioners apply forms of theatre that are specific to their history, community and culture. This is to be welcomed and is not denied by how I have chosen to locate Boal in this work.

A discipline?

While arguing that applied theatre has a necessarily wide reach, the action of writing about it will inevitably develop boundaries that are more distinct. Writing a book can lead to the emergence of the idea of a 'discipline', even when the strictness that this term implies is disavowed. I want therefore briefly to compare it to other 'disciplines' that use the word 'applied'. Whereas applied theatre belongs to the communities in which it is practised, it cannot escape the fact that it has strong roots inside universities and educational establishments. Its place in the academy must therefore be examined.

> Applied mathematics
> Applied anthropology
> Applied physics
> Applied theatre?

These subjects are, therefore, not *mathematics*, nor *anthropology*, nor *physics,* nor *theatre,* but something else. In all of them 'applied' becomes a critical word that condemns and at the same time pleads with the 'non-applied' cousin. It condemns in that the related disciplines are by implication disconnected from the 'real'. They are presented as ivory-tower abstracts. 'Applied' is added to bring the sheltered out of their comfortable buildings – theatres or lecture halls – into the world. It is the term that in the words of social historian Mike Finn 'emancipates the academic from the ivory tower by forcing him or her to confront' real people and real situations (Finn, 2001, p. 17). The 'applied' disciplines appear to fight the esoteric with the used, worn, worked or honed. They champion the practical against the obtuse. However, the word 'applied' also pleads with the 'non-applied' disciplines to legitimise practices that have been kept out of the academies or have struggled to justify their place in them. It petitions them to be considered a part of mathematics, anthropology, physics or theatre and competes with an argument that too often dismisses the *applied* disciplines as opposites to the *pure*. This argument contends that they are not suitable subjects for the

17

academies but the lesser, applied versions of the 'real'. The 'applied' therefore do not only choose to go beyond the building, condemning those that stay inside. They also remain on the outside, kept there by the action of those within.

This ambivalent position compels theatre practitioners to ask whether *applied theatre* is really a useful category if it forces theatre into the company of the sciences of practical use. Are we comfortable with the instrumental intent of that governing verb? Is theatre a practice that needs to be forced out or liberated from its tower? Or does the verb mean that these applied disciplines are separate from and not a freed version of the non-applied other? How does this applied theatre relate to *theatre*? Is theatre squashed by a prefatory word that says its value depends on who it is done *by* and not for what it *is*? Can the critique of abstraction be justified when it is possible to show that all theatre belongs to, grows from, responds to, and cries against the contexts in which it is found? There is a great deal of scholarship to show that performance is minutely tied into and active within the societies in which it operates (see for example Case and Reinelt, 1991; Colleran and Spencer, 1998; Reinelt, 1996). Is it ever so utterly disconnected that it only exists as an irrelevant activity hermetically sealed within the boundaries of well-funded regional theatres, performance venues or university campuses? Mathematics can be understood as an abstraction from real objects to a system of symbols. In this case, the 'applied' word could be a means to reconnect the symbolic system to those objects. But does theatre operate in such a symbolic arena that requires this reconnection? Augusto Boal plays interestingly with this idea:

> Before Pythagoras, adding sacks of rice and beans was easy: sacks stayed still, not exhibiting a will of their own. But how can you add up fifteen cows and seven bulls, all ravenous? Animals, not having the patience for algebra or other philosophies, wanted to graze: which is what they were born for. Pre-Pythagorean arithmetic suffered from such bovine hunger: calculations came out wrong, on the account of an impatient cow or wandering bull.
>
> Pythagoras separated the number from the thing numbered, and human thought took a giant leap forward. (Boal, 2001, pp. 342–3)

The 'applied' word helps it take a huge leap back. Back to the bovine? Linking disciplines to their real-world past. This evolutionary view is one of the inspirations behind a tendency to see applied theatre as a recall to a past theatre practice that was more intricately connected to the realities of people's daily lives. Again Boal:

> In the beginning the theater was the dithyrambic song: free people singing in the open air. The carnival. The feast. Later, the ruling classes took possession of the theater and built their dividing walls. (Boal, 1979, p. 119)

In this definition, applied theatre becomes an exercise in breaking those dividing walls. 'Applied' refers to an act that takes theatre practices out of the obscure black boxes and brings them back to the 'open air'.

However, this turn to the past is too easy. The idea that 'applied' implies a 'connection' is positive because it takes it away from a more direct and crude instrumentality. However, we should be wary of the idea of a return. Evolutionary models too easily permit the belief that research into communities that have vibrant performance practices can teach us about lost rituals of our own. They support divisions between the modern and the savage, which need to be strongly countered as an easy excuse for racism. Applied theatre, although it accepts the idea of a reconnection to the community, should be understood as a contemporary theatre practice that has many different histories and varied rationales depending on where it is happening. To subsume it within a discourse of a longing for an idyllic 'simpler' past denies the complexity of its operation in the moment. This is not to dismiss outright the idea that theatre practice might have changed its role and shifted its relation to the 'people'. Applied theatre in Burkina Faso, Brazil, Sri Lanka and the UK are all practices that use forms, ideas and approaches that have a strong affiliation with the present, and a complex connection to their different pasts. They are not simply evidence of their closeness to an imagined history that only we in the 'developed world' have had the privilege to move through.

The applied disciplines are creating practice in response to a critique that they are too isolated from the communities in which they exist. In addition, they are creating strong theoretical roots to

19

demonstrate that they are disciplines in their own right and not poor relations of the non-applied cousins. Although it is easy to see a return to some mythical origin in these practices, I believe it is more productive to understand them within the dynamics of the different disciplines and the demands of a very utilitarian age. This is the pragmatics and anti-idealism I speak of above. The current discourses of usefulness, relevance, evidence-based practice and value for money are as much a backdrop to the term 'applied theatre' as our desire to burst into dithyrambic song. In using the term 'applied', I am clearly accepting the logic of much of that harsh utilitarianism. However, it is still only a preface to the 'theatre'. Somehow, that *art form* must tangle with the constraints that the prefatory word implies. The problems that ensue in that mix are of course the central concerns of this book.

Disclaiming the mantle: the act of applying

The *act of applying* takes the theatre practitioner or researcher into a number of different academic disciplines, social practices and research fields. The theatre engages with the discourses and approaches in these settings but cannot claim expertise in them. We will always be external to these changing and historically specific debates. Applied theatre comes to psychology, development and prison education (to name some of the areas encountered in this book) but cannot speak for or speak from those fields. We are only ever visitors within the disciplines into which we apply our theatre. This is in the same way that we are only ever invited by the prison governor, the development agency or the refugee group into their setting. We may be familiar with the theoretical debates that inform the practices in these places but we exercise that knowledge from a particular position. We are not expert in these areas nor should we seek to be. One of applied theatre's strengths is in its status as the outsider, the visitor and the guest.

20

This book could have chosen a range of sites to illustrate arguments and debates within applied theatre. I make no apologies for the fact that the examples of application are dependent on the peculiarities of my practical experience and are in no way definitive. They are used to demonstrate the problems of application more than offer an authoritative critique of prison education policy or development theory. The invisibility of the object and the agent as discussed previously means that applied theatre should concentrate on the mechanics of the process, not the specifics of the place. We need to develop a strong sense of critical understanding in these fields, but do so as outsiders to them. The disciplines we meet are historically situated and applied theatre can only engage with that particular moment. It must do so recognising that the practices and ideas that it encounters are contingent. Prison education policy, as is noted in chapter two, shifts historically and artists have engaged and will continue to engage with certain instants in that debate as it is realised in practice. Chapter two is therefore more about the problems of applying theatre than the peculiarities of the philosophy of prison work programmes in the late 1990s. We must be constantly aware that the *act of applying* is an unfinished process that encounters situations that are themselves evolving and not fixed examples of social practice.

The above is stated as a disclaimer; an apology for the inevitable crudeness that emerges in the analysis of certain practices by the non-expert. I am not a prison psychologist, development policy theorist or war trauma analyst, but a theatre practitioner meeting these disciplines at certain moments in their own evolution.

Bewilderment?

There was nothing a crowded, bewildering school could offer me that I could not find in his gracious house. 'All I have to do is watch [...] Watch what you do. That way I can really learn.' [...] So I watched him, I watched him unendingly, all the time, and learned to become what I am. (Gunesekera, 1994, p. 43)

'Bewilderment' in the subtitle is used throughout the book in many different but connected ways. It was first encountered in research into the state of the newly released prisoner who, having suffered a form of sensory deprivation during his or her imprisonment, is 'bewildered' by the massive stimulation that a new-found freedom can provide (see chapter two). The multiple demands of the free world can have a staggering effect upon a person who has just left prison, with its withering effect on the senses. The term in this case has a sense of both incapacitating the ex-inmate and 're-capacitating' through the introduction of a new experience. Bewilderment thus indicates the debilitating dazzle of that experience and the way that a perplexing situation can stimulate. Bewilderment in the context in which it is used in the book does not indicate passivity in the face of a problem, therefore, but rather that transitory state between awe and the struggle to comprehend.

In a number of chapters 'bewilderment' is used to refer to an engagement with theatre practice and research. It is offered as the perplexed condition of the researcher and practitioner as they seek to understand theatre projects in unusual locations or with troubled communities. Rather than being dismissed as a problem, it is welcomed because it counters the over-easy and often stifling effect of certainty. The state of bewilderment is a shorthand for the importance and positive effect of amazement, fascination and doubt. It is the stimulus for critical and questioning research. I argue that this condition is what has maintained the desire of many practitioners to continue working in applied theatre and to strive for answers. It is what produces the best self-reflective writing. The 'beyond' part of the subtitle, however, hints that bewilderment of necessity is a state that people aim to move through. Certainty is still desired, and the book hopes to debate deliberately between doubt and clarity. Bewilderment is thus the position of the theatre-maker who has conducted a piece of work in a community and struggles to find the words that can appropriately articulate the experience. S/he and perhaps the participants are dazzled by the experience, but descriptions fail to capture the full scope of that effect. As emphasised above, this incapacity stimulates a desire for answers. It prompts action and enquiry and in no way implies resignation. Whereas many people do speak with confidence about the way theatre works in community settings, this book starts from the belief that holding onto a memory of bewilderment is a creative and positive impulse, not an admission of the lack of depth or maturity in the field.

Bewilderment is also used to define an experience central to the lives of the many different communities in which applied theatre is practised. It is created by the state of transition between places or times. It is an emotional state that occurs negatively in dislocation and positively in a search for a place of comfort. It is familiar to communities affected by war, violence, exclusion and oppression. If culture is a web that holds and connects people into familiar systems of understanding (Geertz, 1973, p. 5), then damage to those threads, minutely or completely, leads to misconnections, desperate attempts at reconnection or total disconnection. A shattered community is often in the process of moving through bewilderment. These tears are exhibited in groups and individuals struggling to find meaning in their actions and their wider lives: whether that is in their family relations, in transitions to and from prison, in displacement across countries or in the dangerous process of moving through adolescence. The moments of bewilderment are the shock of the new and the loss of the familiar, or the constant, destructive and unsettling process of having opportunities restricted and denied. In the same way that the 'bewildered' researcher can be inspired to respond creatively, communities in transition can also be stimulated to develop a range of innovative and powerful strategies to tackle their problems. People living through the debilitating effect of difficult situations are potentially very able to move beyond. Of course, while I am emphasising the potential of bewilderment to spur positive action, at the extremes it must be acknowledged that utter destruction or complete dislocation can lead to a paralysis and inaction. The state of bewilderment does not prompt a single or inevitable response.

People participating in or watching theatre for the first time often face bewilderment. It is an activity with new physical and emotional demands, that can dis-locate bodies and disrupt accustomed patterns of behaviour. However, it can also be a process that reminds one of or recalls the familiar by recreating forgotten actions or webs of understanding. The strength with which a displaced community seeks to maintain cultural practices can be an attempt to overcome bewilderment. A theatre workshop with prisoners can be a break from previous 'cultural practices', thus causing a momentary sense of confusion. A shift from certainties may be a positive process for some communities, whereas a return to certainties may be the desire of others.

This book in a small way traces the struggle to understand theatre programmes that are based within communities and institutions and in areas that are affected by bewilderment. Although this state can imply a great deal of hurt and damage, it is also considered as a powerful impetus to people's struggle to make sense of their lives. It is also of course the inspiration behind much of the writing presented here. It would have been impossible to sustain enquiry from a basis of absolute clarity. While *applied* might be the prefatory word to 'theatre' therefore, *bewilderment* is the 'preface' to the book.

Introduction
'Making a break for it'

I was trapped inside what I could see, what I could hear, what I could walk to without straying from my undefined boundaries, and in what I could remember from what I learned in my mud-walled school. (Gunesekera, 1994, p. 30)

In theatre any break stimulates. (Boal, 1979, p. 170)

Success in gaining work in theatre is called a 'break'. A 'lucky break', a 'well-earned break' – but a break all the same. It isn't called a mend.

Applied theatre started for me in the world of prisons and the criminal justice system. It represented a break, but not in the sense that it was a first opportunity, rather it created a split with my previous experience of community or political theatre. Entering prison forced me to question one set of practices while quite abruptly starting another. The very structure of a prison ensures that this will happen. You cross a gate and enter a world with its own set of conventions and procedures. Of course, the break for me was a hairline compared to the disruption faced by prisoners and their families. For many inmates, this tear will never mend, for others, it forms a visible scar under their behaviour and for others still, it heals creating a (perhaps worryingly) smooth relationship between their life in prison and their life outside. This re- or dis-location causes one version of the 'bewilderment' in the title of this book. Mine was of course a minor bewilderment compared to that suffered by a prisoner. As is explained in the preface, bewilderment refers to both the disruptions faced by various populations or communities as they shift in place and time, and the questions that emerge from the re-location of theatre forms to new arenas. Bewilderment is a perplexed state created by transition where that movement can include the shift to practising a new form of theatre, the practice of that theatre in a different setting and the dislocation of communities caused by exclusion, violence, poverty or imprisonment.

My experience of entering a prison was enough of a break to force a reconsideration of past practice and a move into something new. I had no idea at the time that this novel terrain would dominate my theatre practice for the next ten years, nor that the complex negotiations this arena required would frame much of the work that is the basis of this book. This practice started a bewilderment that in turn provoked a desire to search for answers – to move beyond. This book traces that search as it has been experienced through different projects and examples of applied theatre in the UK, Brazil, Burkina Faso and Sri Lanka. The break from the certainties of this opening story reaches a conclusion in the final chapter when another practice demanded an assertion of values and clarity. Echoing the see-saw journey that Baz Kershaw traces in his study of contemporary performance between the programmatic and proudly value-led theatre of Brecht and the diffuse, simulated world of the postmodern Baudrillard (Kershaw, 1999), this book travels between a disavowal of fixed positions and a demand for explicitness in the values driving practice. It is informed theoretically by social constructionism and discourse analysis (Potter and Wetherell, 1987; Potter, 1996; Parker, 1998) where applied theatre is understood to work with a community's constructed accounts of itself and competes with the narratives that are more often created by others. This perspective insists that there is no account, story or description that is anything more than an incomplete interpretation, and that therefore one cannot automatically claim authority over another. Although this approach is acutely sceptical about the rhetoric constructed around certain social practices, it also stimulates a pragmatic adoption of certain discourses to explain theatre to non-theatre audiences. This is the 'visitor in the discipline' position that I discussed in the preface. Simultaneously, however, this constructed and strongly relativist view is challenged by a commitment to the radical humanism of educationalists such as Paulo Freire (Freire, 1970) and the theatre director Augusto Boal (Boal, 1979). A belief in the necessity for social change and a commitment to notions of justice, human rights and equality can never quite be extinguished by an assertion that those values are historically specific, partial and relative to the conventions of a particular cultural context.

26

Although the story I start with here at first tips the balance in favour of the interpretative, discourse-sensitive relativism, the book ends with an account of a project that was followed by tragedy four months after it ended: the rehabilitation centre for child soldiers where the project took place was attacked and twenty-nine people were killed. This massacre of young people, many of whom had been project participants, swings the argument firmly back to one that demonstrates an affinity with modernist notions of justice, rights and responsibility. A colleague recently reported how she met parents who showed pictures of their sons from this theatre project, insisting that this was proof that they were still alive. My colleague was part of the Red Cross team that had to tell them that they were mistaken. However much I sympathise with a view that reality is socially constructed, and oppose imposition of one community's values upon another, this incident prompts the final chapter to shift towards a demand for a limit to relativism. Those young people did die, it was not 'just another story', and it was unequivocally wrong. This, however, is a story from a 'youth training camp' for child soldier surrendees in the hill country region of Sri Lanka. This is the end of the book. To get there I must return to the beginning and the beginning was in a prison famous for its own troubles.

Strangeways

My second ever project in prison was to run, with a group of colleagues, a series of workshops in a classroom in pre-riot Strangeways. This was the local adult male remand prison in Manchester, notorious for having a major riot in 1990. My first experience had been as a teacher of English in Galle Prison, Sri Lanka. Although that experience is not discussed here, theatre in the context of Sri Lanka as mentioned briefly above, is the subject of the last chapter of this book. At the time of this second project, I was co-directing a group called the 'anti-Poll-Tax' or APT cabaret. We toured to anti-Poll-Tax groups across the north-west of England with a celebratory thirty-minute set that included a mix of sketch, song and agitprop. The Poll Tax was the popular name for the Community Charge, a new funding system for local authorities introduced by the Conservative Government in 1990. It demanded an equal levy from each voter taking no account of ability to pay and led to a widespread campaign of non-payment. Our cabaret became a familiar opening salvo during a range of political meetings, broadly enjoyed by audiences and either tolerated or belittled by the 'serious' political activists. Our songs and sketches highlighted aspects of the struggle and added a touch of humour to the demand for a countrywide revolt. Non-payment was widely viewed as being highly successful, and represented an impressive example of organised disobedience contributing to social change. This was a political protest that, rare amongst its contemporaries, actually won. Although I take pride in being part of an inspiring movement, for me personally the campaign lost much of its authority and clarity after the riots in Trafalgar Square on 31 March 1990. This was a major national demonstration in London where a carnival atmosphere amongst nearly two hundred and fifty thousand people ended in major riots around the centre of the capital. Whoever was to blame for these, and however melodic were the songs we wrote condemning the police, a celebration was turned into a battle. Not a battle in the literal bricks and boulders of the riot, but in the opportunistic and partial stories that all factions created afterwards to batter each other and bolster themselves. The Trafalgar Square chaos created for me a personal dissonance between the music urging rebellion and a memory of fear, glass and blood. I am not denying the importance of the riot, nor condoning the violence of the police, but questioning the ease with which all sides constructed their 'accounts' of the day. Claim fought counter claim, each naively and dishonestly asserting its truth.

The riot was also an event that coincided (to the same weekend) with the explosion in Her Majesty's Prison, Manchester (or 'Strangeways'). This was the longest and most damaging riot in British prison history, leading to a major commission on prison reform (see Woolf and Tumin, 1991). Politically, personally, theatrically and violently many moments simultaneously became broken, confused

28

and interrelated. My theoretical/theatrical positions and practice were shocked out of their certainties by a reality that was always more slippery and bewildering.

I had already done the project in prison by the time the two riots happened. They acted to stamp home the discomfort I felt after the workshops in the prison. 'I'm going to do some workshops in Strangeways. Do you want to come?' 'But once we enter that space we collude with the oppressive practices within it', I replied. Of course, we always report ourselves to be more eloquent than we are, and in our heads we wish we had been more eloquent than we were. At this point, I have a blank. I cannot remember the argument that proceeded from here. All I know is that it persuaded me in. My suspicions were formed by a clarity that my politics had at that time. Anti-Poll-Tax work was drawing very clear lines in the sand. There were facts – we could not pay – and there were actions that arose directly from them – we will not pay. Our theatre celebrated, sang and dreamt within these precise boundaries. Boundaries from which every chapter in this book both tentatively makes a break and occasionally is forced to reassert. Prison was, I thought, drawn along similarly defined lines. There were facts – I cannot remember what I thought they were now – and there were subsequent actions – you do not cross the gate. On entering a space you collude with the abuses of power that are exercised within it. It was all blindingly, blissfully and unquestionably simple.

Of course, that week in prison kicked those sandy lines in my face. And I have been doing prison theatre with a memory of those bleary eyes ever since. The work then could only be a series of fumbling attempts to see some kind of shape, to make out new boundaries – and dream of the wonderfully straight lines of those Poll-Tax days.

Theatre Bully

So, why has prison theatre been such a bully to my neat theatrical sensibilities? Why does it now provide the context for many of the questions that I ask of applied theatre? In that first week, it immediately generated doubts about some of the principles behind a socially engaged theatre that I thought I understood. Questions sprang up through every game and exercise. Suddenly we were running workshops in a double-cell classroom, with a diverse group of men, aged between twenty and fifty. They were constituents of an audience, an imagined 'people' (Boal, 2001, p. 240) that political theatre so often hopes for but rarely ever reaches. We were forced to ask exactly what sort of theatre should be done here. How in prison do we use theatre to create a celebration with individuals who may have robbed others of joy? How do we deal seriously with issues, when all the group wanted to do was play? How do we work in fantasy, when some of the group's fantasies have been performed in an abusive reality? How do we theatricalise prison's mundanity? How do you create a relevant theatre in a space in which the most forbidden action is escape? I had spent many years condemning a theatre of mindless escapism and suddenly it became the radical counterpart to physical incarceration. Theatre of liberation and escapist theatre were simultaneously part of the same project. This confusion of neat categories is returned to frequently during the book, and helps define many of the arguments that are made. The struggle to overcome that confusion is the slow move beyond bewilderment.

One of my political and community theatre principles had been the importance of the concept of 'giving voice'. Theatre gave voiceless communities an opportunity to speak out. An enjoyable component of the anti-Poll-Tax cabaret had been the simple exercise in voicing dissent. I do not deny that these are relevant aspirations, important actions or possible outcomes for theatre projects. However, in the context of Strangeways prison, we very quickly needed to move beyond the limited notion of 'voicelessness'. In theatre workshops in this context, we struggled to find a place between the desire to

30

challenge the abusive rhetoric of certain voices and enabling others to find theirs for the first time. Hearing the words of some, whether it was in scenes, in descriptions of still images, in movement or writing, could too easily be implicated in the silencing of others. The danger of the 'voice' being seen as a singular construct in community or applied-theatre work is taken up in a discussion of theatre in conflict situations later in chapter five. Here in Strangeways, theatre as a means to offer an individual a voice was mixed very rapidly with a desire to challenge some of what we heard. Abusive, racist and violent voices sang out with the creative, hurt and silenced. 'Giving a voice' became an ethically complex problem, rather than an easily offered solution.

Another principle, similarly challenged, was that participating in theatre developed people's ability to 'act for themselves'. It was an art form that 'empowered'. This seemed particularly relevant to a prison context that severely restricts any right that a person may have to take decisions or make choices. The building, the routine and the time spent there deliberately thwart a sense of subjectivity. However, simply positioning 'Prison Theatre' as a bold attempt to rekindle the prisoner as social actor naively missed the complex relationship that previous 'actions' had to a prisoner's current situation. For a man who had abused, we had to situate the work in the limitations of one's ability and right to act as much as in our desire to empower. As with the notion of 'voice', singular and fixed notions of empowerment were unhelpful. The work could not seek simply to give power. It had also to question the uses of it. For those who had unquestioningly used a variety of positions of power to inflict pain, we wanted perhaps to dis-empower. For those that had been damaged by their personal history and social prejudice, we wanted to offer some sense of control. Sometimes however these were the same person. Prison theatre from these first moments had to be as much about questioning how power was exercised as it was about the process of empowerment.

So, after a week that shocked, inspired and confused, we desperately searched for new models. The five days of workshops had seen a six-foot Liverpudlian quietly crochet through a bitter domestic scene and an elderly Asian man play an assertive daughter to a Rastafarian father. They had heard a senior London prisoner who had

31

been moved to Manchester as a punishment say that this was the best week he had had in seven years. All this might have been convincing evidence of theatre's impact, but it did not provide an appropriate language to articulate it. The language of empowering oppressed communities and celebrating opposition fitted neatly at moments and was glaringly inappropriate at others. In the same way that triumphant anti-Poll-Tax songs jarred with the Trafalgar Square riot, theatre workshops in this prison created a dissonance with over-neat frameworks for 'radical theatre'. An explanatory system of 'giving voice' or 'empowering the oppressed' had to be firmly renegotiated so that the work continued to make sense. The bewilderment forced a search for new places and different disciplines that could offer some way of understanding the work. Appropriate 'talk' about theatre in this context was needed to convince ourselves and, in addition, to explain what we were doing to certain constituent parts of our new audience. Articulating 'why theatre in prisons' needed a clarity for the wary prison governors and officers, even when we did not have it for ourselves.

Of course making a break from one model does not mean that the practice forges original models on its own. We sought out a framework that could contain and explain some of the doubts that had been encountered. A convenient oppositional framework was found in the world of the Probation Service. Competing with the then Conservative Home Secretary Michael Howard's vision that prison worked was a movement that asked 'What Works?' (McGuire, 1995). This combination of rehabilitation enthusiasts, probation staff and criminal psychologists maintained that through an analysis of programmes for offenders, they could discover those that reduced recidivism. Through this process and the presentation of the results at a yearly international conference, they sought out categories of positive and effective practice. These approaches, they argued, could then be harnessed by agencies that sought change in the behaviour of prisoners and probation clients. The most highly regarded intervention within this field was a form of cognitive behavioural group work that was based on a belief that individuals by changing their thinking, could change their behaviour (see Harland, 1996; McGuire, 1995; Rose, 1998 for examples). These programmes aimed to explore with

32

participants, the links between actions and personal reflection or justification. The community involved in the 'What Works?' debate sought to demonstrate that, appropriately implemented, this type of group work could lead to fewer convictions for 'clients' in the future. It was an arena of practice that very quickly provided a point of departure in the search for models to make sense of prison theatre work, and it continues to be a reference for much of the writing in this book. At that time, a field that believed in the potential of changing the 'offender' in a criminal justice system that more often regarded 'criminality' as a permanent personality defect, provided us with inspiration.

However, this field was not only useful because of its belief in the potential for human change. Cognitive and behavioural psychology also uses many quasi-theatrical references and these became markers that we used to explain our practice. For example, group work for prisoners and probationers used behaviour rehearsal, modelling, and role play (see for example Rose, 1988; Hollin, 1990; Goldstein and Glick, 1994) as component parts of their courses. An offending behaviour group therefore might ask members to recreate offences, show arguments with peers or practice new ways of responding to certain difficult situations. The social learning theory that underpins much of this therapeutic work is based on the writings of Bandura, who argued that human action is a process that moves from observing others to 'performing' new behaviours (Bandura, 1977, p. 24). These common references therefore provided a structure around which we could build a way of understanding the place of theatre within the criminal justice system. We moved with confidence to this field, unsure at first how it related to the theatre that we practised. The desire for answers made us make what was at first a discursive shift. The next few years were spent learning the language and then the practice of offending-behaviour group work. Our new home allowed us to draw some tentative lines around our projects. It gave us a framework for analysis, discussion and advocacy. The deliberate learning of a discourse was for me the first distinctive act of practising an 'applied theatre'. We explicitly took a form of social practice and constructed our techniques and programmes from within its boundaries and frames of understanding. Applied theatre in this

33

version appeared to be an act of 'simple translation'. It involved theatre practitioners entering a field and negotiating with a particular set of theories and approaches, which of course – as we were to discover later – were only one particular, partial approach to rehabilitation.

This experience immediately taught many lessons for the development of theatre projects that sought to 'apply' themselves. For example, often when examining areas of 'applied theatre' the theatre work is seen as central, and the meetings, promotions and demonstrations that surround it are viewed as secondary. All the planning and explaining are 'mere' preliminaries to the most important moment of the workshop or performance. This results in a concentration on the 'practice' and a sidelining of those aspects of the work that actually take up more time. What is assumed to be the heart of the work (those workshops, performances and plays) is rewarded disproportionately with attention and analysis. The painstaking action of promotion and advocacy becomes sidelined and undervalued. The actual act of translating the work to the new discipline is not analysed. Whereas I hope that this book shows that applied theatre must be more than 'translation', I believe it is important to emphasise that in this example there developed a variety of complementary practices. This means that we did not separate out and create hierarchies of certain moments. A meeting explaining prison theatre work to a group of probation officers was as much part of the practice, as a drama workshop with a group of prisoners. The development of a discourse around theatre and 'offending behaviour group work' (see Priestley and McGuire, 1985) that was performed in meetings, in workshops, at criminal justice conferences and in prison officer's canteens was a total package. It was all practice. Of course it adapted, shifted and was sensitive to different audiences, but in the early years of my experience in this work speaking the language of the arena was as important as the projects undertaken within it.

Gradually this hesitant speech gave way to fluency; it was embedded, learnt, imprinted in minds and on the page (Thompson, 1999a). It was regurgitated, reworked and reformulated to perform to a range of occasionally sceptical listeners. It became our ethos and way of comprehending the work. It generated a foundation from which new projects derived their coherence and theoretical justification. It was the rhetorical packaging of our theatre work that played well to the 'What works?' audience. It is important to emphasise that we were always theatre people interpreting and performing an approach, but also that performance was often unacknowledged in an apparent desire to belong to this new field rather than maintain the status of outsider.

The new lines in the sand gave a number of years of comfort. They eased my bleary eyes and started to take me beyond my initial bewilderment. In 1992, with my colleague Paul Heritage, I set up the Theatre in Prisons and Probation or TIPP Centre, and through that organisation we created programmes on offending behaviour, anger management, drugs, bullying and employment (Thompson, 1999a). Each interacted with the practices of the related fields and sought to enhance them with the techniques of participatory theatre. All the projects borrowed from a radical theatre practice with techniques predominantly drawn from the work of Augusto Boal (Boal, 1992, 1995) but now adapted to the requirements of cognitive behavioural group work practice. In an anger-management course created for Greater Manchester Probation Service, for example, we used the tableaux work of Boal's Image Theatre (Boal, 1992, p. 164), but shifted its focus so that it was used to reveal the thought processes behind each moment leading to violence. Image Theatre gave groups a controlled method for examining the building of anger. In the offending behaviour workshop, we used images to break up narratives around crime, and then small Forum Theatre scenes (Boal, 1992, p. 17) for the groups to practice 'new behaviours'. Boal was in the background and the exercises were explained with a criminal justice rehabilitation vocabulary. We adapted the practice and learnt new languages that were used both because they opened doors – performed – and also because they gave coherence to the work.

One of the major questions posed at this time was how we could maintain a strong theatrical accent when engaged in or speaking about the work, without losing our criminal-justice credibility: how to negotiate that position of guest or visitor in the field. For this to happen theatre processes could not be alternatives to rehabilitation projects but they had to be promoted as enhancements, extensions and improvements to group work practice. Once comfortable within the discourse, there was a desire to push its boundaries. We would, for example, argue that participation engaged in ways that sedentary courses did not; metaphor created different resonances, connections and memories that the literal could not; role plays created three-dimensional discursive acts that extended and perhaps complicated the explanations of behaviour that relied on speech alone. Offender rehabilitation framed all, but we stretched ourselves out practically and discursively within the boundaries that it set.

The work became particularly interesting when we noticed that staff members from within criminal justice institutions were picking up our language. We started to hear a potentially synthesised discourse emerging. The TIPP Centre always insisted that non-theatre staff could replicate its projects and workshops – a clear reference to Boal's belief in training and working with 'non-actors'. To this end, probation and prison officers were trained to run most of the programmes. This is still happening in 2002 with the TIPP Centre training staff from the new Youth Offending Teams (YOTs) to use a drama based offending-behaviour workshop. This desire continues but it also raises some of the most important questions for this work.

The central concern is to ask what happens in this process to the theatre practice itself. Does it become so corrupted by the criminal-justice accent brought by these staff that it looses some kind of 'quality'? Or does our theatre accent only really amount to a lilt that masks what is otherwise a common criminal-justice approach? Or have we entered some middle, synthesised zone and are thus promoting a new grammar of practice? In this desire to train others, has our 'radical heritage' been diluted beyond recognition? As I had worried before that early visit, had entering the discursive place, meant that we were colluding? Had we forgotten that we were not criminal psychologists? Were we in fact pushing any boundaries at all? One of the problems for applied theatre is the difficulty in understanding where it ends; where the process of 'applying theatre' finally becomes the moment of 'applied theatre'. If it is only an act of translation, when does it finish? We need to examine whether this field in fact dies at the moment it becomes fully incorporated into a particular social arena. When we heard the prison officers using some of our terms in describing their group work, had we achieved our aims? Was the absence of a boundary between the criminal justice and the theatre practice evidence of success, or in being fully applied did it no longer exist? Does theatre become truly applied when you cannot see the points of application? Had we finally disappeared in the rush to get through those gates or was this 'wishful thinking', hiding a process that in fact should never be completed?

These questions reflect many of the concerns that will be echoed and commented on throughout this book. However, when they were first encountered, it was necessary to return to an inspiration behind the theatre practice to start to discover how we could approach them. As I have noted above, the work in prison theatre borrowed many techniques from the practice of Augusto Boal. The shift from the didactic anti-Poll-Tax cabaret had required a borrowing of participatory theatre forms that permitted groups to create their own performances. However adapting the different forms had not always included staying faithful to their purpose. Many of the projects described within these pages debate similar adaptations of Boalian theatre. In chapter three, for example, an analysis of the work of Atelier Théâtre Burkinabé in Burkina Faso directly examines both the role of Boal and how the anxieties about losing sight of original principles affect many interpretations of applied theatre. At the point in the example given here, a return to Boal was made possible by a visit to his homeland. It was prison theatre in Brazil that therefore provided another break. A reminder that the techniques that we borrowed had a principled intent.

A break in Brazil – from behaviour to citizenship? The Salão Nobre

Having worked with colleagues to develop the cognitive behavioural group work programmes in the UK for five years, an opportunity arose to work on a number of prison projects in Brazil. These were all initiated and directed by my colleague Paul Heritage from Queen Mary, University of London. In 1997 a series of workshops were to be run in Carandiru prison in the city of São Paulo. Carandiru, I was told while touring the institution for the first time, holds more inmates than any other prison in Latin America. Pride in the size of your prison may seem a strange device for impressing visitors, but it was an immediate reminder that criminal-justice systems are constructed around rhetorical devices that often have little to do with impact on crime. Absorbed by the boundaries created around work in Britain, it was hard at that time to see that the 'offending behaviour' discourse was perhaps another rhetorical device that masked a practice that had a similarly ambiguous impact. With my British and Brazilian colleagues, we were there to run a pilot programme of theatre-based AIDS/HIV education workshops. This was the middle point of a three-year project between the University of Campinas, the Fundação Professor Dr Manoel Pedro Pimentel (FUNAP – the São Paulo state foundation responsible for work and education in the prisons), the São Paulo state prison system and the TIPP Centre. The project went on to be run across the state prison system and in 2002 it has become the 'Staging Human Rights' programme replicated in many states across Brazil. This initiative is now directed by People's Palace Projects at Queen Mary, University of London, and has sought to use theatre to stimulate debate on issues of Human Rights in all sections of the Brazilian criminal justice system.

Our venue in 1997 was the Salão Nobre – a huge cavern of a hall, with a high balcony at one end and a stage at the other – an opera house without the seats. The protestant evangelical prisoners were working on the balcony and there were various inscriptions on the walls quoting the Bible. There was a confusion in the space as to whether it functioned as a theatre or a church. In a prison in Rio de Janeiro called Lemos Brito there is a similar hall (with seats this time) which again is both theatre and church. While watching a theatre workshop there in 1999, I noticed a huge sign hung across the stage:

Tema: A Glória da segunda Casa
(*Theme: The Glory of the second House*)

Divisa: A Glória desta última casa será maior do que a da primeira [...] e neste lugar darei a paz.
(*Slogan: The glory of this last house will be better than that of the first* [...] *and that place will give peace.*) (NB: 'house' is another word for prison.)

Although a reference to Solomon's second temple at Jerusalem, I could not help understanding it as an ironic demand for renovation and an allusion to the confusion in the identity of the 'house'. Church, theatre or prison? Could the second house – theatre – ever give peace? These two halls seemed to hark back to some original glory, some original intent which was now long since forgotten. Peeling walls and puddles of water in both the Salão Nobre and the hall in Rio marked the caves as faded echoes of some past that no one seemed to remember. Suddenly theatre in these spaces hinted at that past, and also reminded me that 'some original intent' within the practice of prison theatre in the UK was starting to be forgotten. These workshops became the context to take us back to an 'original glory' when prison theatre was done struggling through 'bleary eyes' rather than the cool 'cognitive behavioural' certainty. Of course, one echo that was loud here in Brazil was the work of the educationalist Paulo Freire and the theatre director Augusto Boal, two Brazilians who in developing a questioning pedagogy and a problem-posing theatre had inspired much of the prison work in the first place.

The Salão Nobre thus played a suitably ambiguous role in framing the meanings held in that day. Outsiders came to work inside, gringos with Brazilians, white with black, and the free with the captive. All powerful dichotomies in their own right, and here once again lines that were confused in the activity of the workshop. After the initial introductions, the session took off. Approximately thirty prisoners, two British theatre workers, two Brazilian theatre students and two prison officials. Two hours of participatory theatre on AIDS, HIV and sexually transmitted diseases. Still images were created by the prisoners out of the bodies of their peers. Images of drug use, conflict and desperation. Images of friendship and hope. Images of the complex life of the prison that I might read in one way and the group might read in another. The tableaux of the present were changed to reveal desires for the future. The group created stories that were interesting for both what they said and what remained unspoken. The silences told as loudly as the narratives that were voiced. The confusing and delightful stories of the Strangeways workshop were replicated in new and specific tales from São Paulo.

The origins of this workshop in Carandiru and of all the prison theatre work that I have been involved with in Brazil can be traced to the work of Paul Heritage in a prison called Papuda in the capital Brasília (see Heritage, 1998a, p. 31). It was the development of projects in this space and subsequent lessons from the workshop in the Salão Nobre that started to shift a perspective on prison theatre work in the UK and make explicit some of the tensions within it. In the first instance, the Papuda and the Salão Nobre projects challenged some of the wider assumptions behind the rehabilitation theories popular in the UK criminal justice system, assumptions that I had taken with me into our applied-theatre prison projects. In Brazil, they were not interested in the broadly cognitive behavioural group work practice from the UK. This in itself reminded us that our practice was a product of a very specific political, ideological and cultural moment. It had no straightforward legitimacy outside that context. Applied theatre needs to be constantly reminded that in the *act of applying* it is meeting a specific moment in the history of a different system of knowledge. Aligning itself too closely with one set of practices relegates the work to one historical moment, making it too easily irrelevant as approaches and ideologies change. In Brazil, prison education and rehabilitation were framed more in the discourses of cultural and human rights. They argued that there was no point in predicating work on the idea of personal change – as ultimately cognitive behavioural work does – if the extreme conditions of poverty that the vast majority of prisoners come from and return to were not transformed. The theatre programme in Brasília became about reconnecting people to their society, not insisting that they could change in isolation from it. The project in Papuda culminated in a performance by prisoners on issues of slavery, oppression on Brazilian ranches, and the racism of the criminal-justice system. These plays were eventually taken out of the prison, to performances for families of prisoners and the prison hierarchy in the Ministry of Justice. In these events the work of Boal was turned on its head, with the elite being petitioned to intervene on

40

stage and solve the problems that they were presented as upholding (see Heritage, 1998a for a fuller description). This process positioned the prisoners as actors and citizens who had the right to ask questions and to debate solutions to some of the central issues in Brazilian society. It confused the neat dichotomy between the citizen and the prisoner. This dichotomy was also – of necessity – confused that day in the Salão.

The break back to Brazil happened therefore both practically and theoretically. It reminded us of the Freirian roots (Freire, 1970) to Boal's work and the need to refocus on those origins. We should not have been so beguiled by the promise of change in cognitive behavioural therapies, to forget that behaviourism often assumes what is the correct solution for the problems in the participant's lives. We should not have been so impressed by the participatory potential of Boal's techniques not to remember that they had an original intent. We needed to refocus on the Freirian concept of 'cultural invasion' (Freire, 1970, p. 161) and be clear that an agenda of change set from the outside is more often an imposition than an act of liberation. In learning a language to get us through certain gates, we had perhaps lost sight of the principles that were, until we returned to Brazil, hidden or unspoken. The break from political cabaret to participatory prison theatre required a challenge to certain tenets of radical theatre but a re-examination of others. We had borrowed from Boal but perhaps allowed some principles to slip – to peel and fade. The tension of turning Boalian theatre into cognitive behavioural group therapy, was therefore not a struggle of adaptation and a neat application, but in places a clash of principle. The desire for 'dialogical cultural action' (Freire, 1970, p. 160) was too often replaced with proscriptions in a criminal justice system that had clear lines between what was right behaviour and wrong behaviour. We enjoyed a dialogue between the forms, but glossed over the fact that one form could too easily become a monologue insisting on what changes the group members should make in their lives.

Translation is never perfect; it is always an act of recreation. We had denied those problems, those 'imperfections', in our enthusiasm for the work. Much of the rehabilitative group work in the UK criminal-justice system presents a behavioural ideal that the group

must reach. The behaviour of the good citizen is written, and the process of the therapeutic group revolves around the participants slowly learning the script. The future, the target, is predetermined. However, the workshop in the Salão Nobre very directly insisted that we could not know what was possible behaviour for another person. The process could therefore, only pose the problem, ask the question and involve people in searching for solutions. As the gringo in Carandiru, it would have been absurd for me to tell the prisoners what sort of citizens they should be. All we could do was involve them in creating their own visions of the way they connected to their society.

Back to Carandiru and the Salão Nobre

AIDS education is all about behaviour. It is often limited to a demand for a very simple behavioural change – 'get people to use condoms'. It was on this point that Carandiru reminded us that behavioural solutions, however simple, could not be given but must be discovered in the process. The tendency to assume that we could identify the problems of our groups in the UK – we knew that their joyriding was 'wrong' – was radically undermined by this experience. The only way that the simple divisions between the group on that day could be breached, was by a pedagogical principle that all we could do was ask questions and learn. The dichotomy between captive and free person, Brazilian and gringo, could only be confused by challenging the assumption about knowledge that this division provides. I did not know what AIDS meant in that prison. The Image Theatre of Boal was used therefore to create versions of the group's reality and give all the opportunity to read what they saw. One participant's image of a guard and a prisoner was read by others as a father and son. This technique enabled multiple readings of images of AIDS to be linked to other narratives and for the group to hint at possible solutions. When one man's AIDS tableau was read by another as a story of hunger caused by the drought in the north-east of Brazil (from where many of these prisoners originated), the new connections, acknowledgements and resonance became a central learning experience – for the whole group.

In Carandiru the education department was not staffed by outside professionals, as is the practice in the majority of Brazilian prisons and certainly all prisons in the UK. Here prisoners were trained to be 'monitors' and they would then teach other prisoners. This was done both because of a sound pedagogical principle and more practically because the prevalence of violence within the institution made it too dangerous to have outside educators working on a permanent basis. Our group that day was made up of prison monitors who because of their position had a degree of power and respect within the prison community. This meant that the work might be sustained after we left by these prisoner-teachers continuing the debates in their own classrooms. Asking questions in this context could provide a breach of the simple, clean divisions that prison walls seek to create. Gringos might ask questions, but prisoners provided answers, which then became questions for other groups of inmates. Having a prearranged behavioural script to pass on – use condoms – would have ensured no dialogue and a reinforcement of the barriers between all these groups.

Use a condom. – We don't have any.
Use a condom. – They are prohibitively expensive for our partners who come to the prison for conjugal visits.
Use a condom. – Wives are sold on conjugal visits to other prisoners to pay off debts and you can't control the condom use of your creditor.
Use a condom. – I'll die from violence long before I die from AIDS.
Use a condom. – Many of us are already HIV positive.

Asking questions is a central part of the structure of this book. This is not through a fear of providing answers but because these questions form a principle of applied-theatre practice. The theatre that is proposed is one that asks, and the breaks that have been made are from practices that have insisted or started to insist that there are definitive answers. I shifted from a didactic anti-Poll-Tax cabaret to the confused prison theatre practice. However, when this too edged towards a model that was aiming to teach people correct ways of behaving, a new break was sought. This was found in a Brazilian reminder of the intent of many of the participatory techniques that we had already been using. The inability to offer even the simplest answer in Brazil was the intimation that theatre should always start from what is a healthy sense of bewilderment.

A final break?

In February 1999 I had another break and I left the TIPP Centre. This gave me the privilege of looking back at the work again. One of the inspiring aspects of prison theatre, as I explained at the beginning of this introduction, was how it disturbed simplistic frameworks and how it played havoc with neat lines of understanding. The learning and practising within the discourse of offending-behaviour group work was a product of this state of confusion. It was a search for new shapes to make the work understandable. However, in occupying a certain discursive arena, it became hard to see beyond that arena. It is hard to see the boundaries of something when you are immersed in it. The transference of the practice back to Brazil made some of those boundaries more visible. Without seeing these edges, we can forget that lines around a field both shape and constrict it. The practice is explained, created and performed from within a restricted field and starts to loose the possibilities offered by others. My new vantage point has allowed me to question whether the apparently 'synthesised' discourse/practice had become a new orthodoxy, and whether in apparent completion, this version of applied theatre had perhaps died. The experience of Brazil was the prompt behind this concern, however only on stepping away again did new possibilities for understanding applied theatre start to emerge.

This new position is the inspiration behind and informs all of the debates in this book. Making the 'final' break permitted reflection on how the boundaries of the 'What works?' movement and the cognitive behavioural field had restricted aspects of the practice. We need to be conscious of how all theoretical and discursive frameworks

44

encountered during applied-theatre programmes can in fact limit as much as they enable. The TIPP Centre was at first attracted by the fact that the offender rehabilitation field challenged the official view that nothing worked and also that it held on to a belief in change. That field inspired but eventually conspired against creative programmes. In a sense, the move through bewilderment increased creativity, but as it was forgotten, some of the innovation permitted by honest uncertainty was lost. For example, the first project of the TIPP Centre, the *Blagg!* offending-behaviour workshop, was created while we discovered what a drama-based offender rehabilitation programme could be (see Thompson, 1995 and 199a for detailed descriptions of this project). I believe this project, created as a process of developing understanding, was more dynamic and impressive than the anger management programme that followed it. The latter project, commissioned by the Greater Manchester Probation Service, lacked the precision of its predecessor because it was created from an over-comfortable foundation of assumed clarity rather than the creative moment of wide-eyed exploration. This all took place in a broader context that has seen the 'what works' field of the early 1990s replaced with a 'this works' instruction emerging from the New Labour government. The questioning process has been completed with a national system of programme accreditation and standardisation. One example of this trend is the publication of a report by Her Majesty's Inspectorate of Probation called 'Evidence Based Practice'. Page fifteen of this document encourages the use of drama in group work programmes. It states that:

> Drama [...] if purposefully and carefully designed and delivered, can address a range of criminogenic needs including:
> * anti-social attitudes, beliefs and values
> * anti-social associates
> * lack of pro-social role models
> * cognitive and interpersonal skills
> * dependence upon alcohol and drugs
> * a sense of achievement and community integration
> * employment
> * social isolation
> * mental health (Chapman and Hough 1998, p.15)

Should this be seen as a victory for applied theatre? Should we cheer? I am not so sure…

Discursive frames can act to iron out confusions and doubts. My anti-Poll-Tax clarity had been translated into a cognitive behavioural clarity about how human behaviour is formed, enacted and relearnt. It assumed that learnt behaviour is stored and reperformed at a later date; it accepted a role theory that says we are but exhibitors of social types; it hoped that if we rehearse something in one space it might be executed in another. It aspired to a form of human agency that could be aroused by theatre and transferred to the real world. It was necessarily optimistic, but at the same time worryingly simplistic. Our confidence in the efficacy of applying theatre to social wounds made it problematically mechanistic. Some of the projects came close to telling people how to behave – to stop stealing cars. This book starts the process of challenging these lines because they are limiting. What started as a partial reading of the practice, became a partial frame in which to develop that practice. The work was in danger of becoming a pale version of what it could be. I believe that now we must re-examine the lines that we had found it necessary to create. We need to rediscover a critical voice to challenge the language and assumptions of the cognitive-behavioural account of applied theatre.

To continue, there needs to be a memory of that initial state of confusion. Sometimes that might mean a return to those practitioners who have inspired; but at other times our bleary eyes must stare resolutely forward. I acknowledge that in the process of rekindling that sense of enquiry, a new and altered clarity might emerge, but the practice of struggling towards new lines is the moment in which rich examples of applied theatre might be forged. By way of polemic, I propose here four positions from which I aim to start this process. These are meant as challenges more to the certainties that I have worked within than to the frameworks to which others might adhere. They are meant to raise some dust to open the 'bleary-eyed searching' that constitutes this book.

1. We need to question role theory. It is reductive, and assumes that role is personally held when it is in fact socially constructed and situational. We adapt our performances from a range of resources,

not by choosing singular roles. We improvise and construct from a multitude of possible performances that are learnt, witnessed and embodied. We do not regurgitate fixed roles.

Applied theatre cannot just be about increasing your 'role repertoire' or creating 'good characters'.

2. We should abandon behaviourism. We should be interested in action, not behaviour. 'Behaviour' implies that humans create their world from the inside out. The world is created within each different situation that arises. Using the word 'action' allows us to interpret human activity as adaptations between people not as scripts emanating from within.

Applied theatre cannot be just about changing 'behaviour'.

3. We need to challenge the primacy given to cognition. Performances do not belong to a creator cognitive God. There is no central Cartesian scriptor sorting and deciding. We perform adaptively within and between situations, people, times and contexts. There is no original cognitive process that is magically exposed by analysing our decision-making, role playing or behaviour.

Applied theatre cannot just be about revealing thought processes, or personal scripts.

4. We need to question the deferred promise of rehearsal. Demonstration of a skill in one place cannot be a guarantor that it will happen elsewhere. We do not simplistically store total interactions for later display. Workshops are not only a preparation for what will happen afterwards, but should be valued for what they are in the present. Perhaps the revolution will not be rehearsed.

Applied theatre cannot just be about practising for the future.

In different ways and in different places, each of these areas will be referred to in the chapters that follow. In the spirit of this enquiry, they do not appear in a neat chronological order. The chapters may deal with them theoretically or, in outlining an area of practice, use them as a point of departure. Chapter one deals most explicitly with notions of behaviour and the way our action is perhaps constructed from the tiniest slivers of behaviour rather than complete roles. This is used to outline a proposal for applied theatre to be understood as the playing with fragments or the 'matter of action' rather than as a social-skills training exercise. The criticism of chapter one is then taken directly into an account of prison-theatre practice on employment-training programmes in chapter two. This account examines the term 'bewilderment' to search for a richer way of framing examples of this practice; one that does not rely on formulations related to applied theatre as a 'rehearsal for the future'. This chapter asks how the moment of the workshop can be understood if it is uncoupled from the assumption that it is only done as a preparation for release. Chapter three shifts focus to examine the adaptations made to Boalian theatre by Atelier Théâtre Burkinabé (ATB), a company in Burkina Faso. It uses concepts taken from debates within interculturalism to examine the relationships between formal adaptations, exchanges and impositions. The fear of the loss of principles of practice outlined here is discussed in relation to how this anxiety can cloud interpretations of unfamiliar examples of applied theatre. Worry about the loss of core values – for example the Freirian desire not to set an agenda for your group – meant that the practice of ATB became judged within inappropriate limits. My suggestion in this introduction that we needed to be reminded of an original intent thus becomes challenged when that sense of purpose becomes a means to criticise unfairly the practice of others.

Chapter four on 'Theatre Action Research' moves away from a precise example of practice to propose ways in which 'playing with action matter' could be adapted as a research method rather than as a method to be researched. This chapter uses the language of the 'action matter' chapter to suggest an approach to analysing community problems or assessing past interventions. The final chapter concentrates on theatre projects in Sri Lanka to ask questions about the ethics of applied-theatre practice. The chapter contends that a discussion of ethics becomes more acutely problematic and simultaneously more necessary in the context of a war. Again, this chapter questions the relationship between a flexible and adaptive vision of applied theatre and one that is governed by clarity of principle or philosophy. This chapter offers the final dance between the power of certainty and the creativity of bewilderment that characterises many of the accounts in this book.

Back to the break

In my work in prison theatre, the most radical moment was not the creation of a way to understand the work, but the actual break from certainties. However, a search for certainties both in the return to Brazil and in the turmoil of Sri Lanka is encouraged, not dismissed. Harking back to Boal and Freire or hoping for an ethics of applied theatre is a vital part of the dance between 'bewilderment and beyond'.

Gaining something in the world of theatre is called a break – not a mend. That move from political cabaret to prison theatre for me created a more vibrant theatre practice. The first projects that I undertook in prison were pursued in a state of bleary-eyed searching – and these I believe now were the most innovative and challenging. The more fixed and clear we found ourselves, the weaker the creative content of our practice. However inversely, that clarity is what enabled the work to prosper in a challenging, retribution-dominated climate. Although it may be that it is in the creases and roughness of doubt that creativity flourished, it is in the translations to certainty that it was sustained. The ironing and smoothing was a process that erased and excluded but also explained and strengthened. This book thus exists in one of those creases, but hopefully also looks beyond. It inevitably smoothes at times, but at others it deliberately breaks and doubts. It jumps in context and style to maintain that sense of question and the belief that boundaries are lines with which we should play.

If theatre were only a skills-training method for probation clients to practice roles that they could then perform in later life, we would loose the complexity of the workshop and performance process as a dynamic, difficult and rich moment in itself. If theatre were simply an opportunity to challenge young people's antisocial attitudes and change their 'cognitive and interpersonal skills', it would lose the possibility for the unexpected, surprising and radically disturbing. In creating a simplistic relationship between the workshop room and the world outside, we restrict the variety of confusions, memories or connections that theatre can stimulate for a range of people. Theatre could be the dissonance between worlds, but it could also be the means to a smooth transition. Theatre can be both opportunity and disruption.

Success in theatre is called a 'break'. I hope the chapters that follow provide a place for lines to be drawn and certainties to be disturbed. I of course welcome challenges to any of the orthodoxies that I create in these pages. Their weaknesses, their creases and roughnesses, are mine and mine alone.

Chapter One
On the matter of action

A mind or consciousness could be seen not as an atomistic singularity but as interwoven within a broader social or cultural or contextual field that includes others. In such a case, an 'I' would be more fuzzy and diffused, less coterminous with the body, more intermeshed within its context, more interdependent. We would talk about selves, actions, and, even, thoughts as less exclusively individual and more inclusively relational, webbed, arrayed, archaeological. (Scheurich, 1997, p. 165)

The [Kathakali] training involves learning new ways of speaking, gesturing, moving. Maybe even new ways of thinking and feeling. New for the trainee, but well known in the tradition of kathakali, ballet, and noh. As in initiation rites the mind and body of each performer are returned toward a state of *tabula rasa* […] ready to be written on in the language of the form being learned. When finished with training, the performer can 'speak' noh, kathakali, or ballet: s/he is 'incorporated' into the tradition, initiated and made one with the body of the tradition. The violence of scarring or circumcision is absent – but deep, permanent psychological changes are wrought. A kathakali performer, a ballet dancer, a noh shite each have their genre-specific ways of moving, sounding, and, I would say, being: they are marked people. (Schechner, 1993, p. 257)

Cognition […] allows us to re-enact, in symbolic form, the little dramatic performances we have selected from the behaviour of others. (Sheldon, 1995, p. 86)

A pattern of marks entering my own stillness. Feeling someone inscribing the soft grey tissue of my brain, writing on water, and rippling my mind. (Gunesekera, 1994, pp. 51–2)

Approaches to applied theatre have tended to view it as promoting personal skills, competencies and role-taking abilities that then become complete resources for the person to use in future interactions. If, however, as I outlined in the introduction, singular roles rarely exist, and our actions cannot be understood as emanating from the person outwards, we need to search for a more complex framework for understanding the work. This chapter will use and challenge the quotations above to argue that we are all in fact 'marked people' who exhibit the patterns created by the 'little dramatic performances' of others, in and through our daily actions. Our bodies and our lives are both shaped and we in turn shape our bodies, giving us the ability to engage with our friends, families and communities. The chapter claims that the process described by Schechner, whereby training of performers in certain traditions is an action akin to scarring, is an extreme and radical version of a more subtle training/learning we all experience. We are not the *tabula rasa* and we would not aspire to such erasure, but different forms of human interaction simultaneously affect and are dependent upon the way we have embodied (mentally and physically) past experience. The chapter seeks to tie this into a vision of human action that is understood to be part of the relational web of interdependence outlined by Scheurich. We are marked; but these contours go beyond our bodies to bind us to wider, shifting networks. They connect outside of ourselves and are 'intermeshed' within a context. By accepting a more 'fuzzy and diffused' understanding of the mind, coupled with an argument that a complex set of marks rather than 'roles' are what become the raw material for action, I believe a richer understanding of the workings of applied-theatre projects can be developed. The approach is thus a recasting of the behaviourism and role theory discussed in the introduction, and of this 'visiting theatre person's' extended dialogue with a cognitive behavioural account of applied theatre encountered in past experience of the work.

The phrase 'action matter' is used to acknowledge that our behaviour is constructed out of embodied potentials, traits and experiences that coalesce into full interactions between people in the moment of their execution. It is used to indicate that this construction is not based on disembodied cognitive processes, but on action that is substantive; it is etched into and exhibited through the shape of our muscles, nerves and tissue. We play with this matter – what Schechner refers to as 'bits of behaviour' – in an endless process of repetition and adaptation creating seemingly unique events (Schechner, 2002, p. 23). Applied-theatre programmes are run with groups of people with different histories of being 'marked'. In the execution of a project, the web of interrelations between groups is examined and new yet fragile interconnections can be built. Applied theatre can be an experience that develops links between people – above, around and through the existing shapes of the participants' lives. It is not the violent process described by Schechner, but in playing with 'bits of behaviour' it can, gently or faintly, mark.

The chapter seeks to expand these arguments so that a broad framework can be developed which will then be used to examine the practices in the later chapters. These lines are drawn here in a series of short paragraphs touching on a range of areas that aim to provide a boundary that can be both tested and stretched. The chapter will start by referring to some of the 'action matter' and 'little performances' that make up my own life. These are of course meant to be illustrative and are in no way special or unique.

Scratching the surface/skin deep

[Palimpsest:] a manuscript on which two or more texts have been written, each one being erased to make room for the next (*Collins Concise Dictionary*, 2001, p. 1079).

A large proportion of my 'behaviour' is constructed with the remnants of 'action matter' that originally appeared in the behaviour of my parents. This is not a history or simple memory or an act of cognitive recall. It is not a glimmer of an interaction; an ancient scene constructed out of picture fragments and barely remembered words. It is not I as a subject creating them as my desired other self. Fathers and mothers, parents, are/were separate, but their past actions become marked on the bodies of their children. Rubbing gently at the interactions, conversations and routines of individuals' daily lives will reveal action phraseology familiar to their parents. For example, my family recognise my father *in* me. Whereas a ballet dancer will have a 'genre-specific way of moving', I, and I would claim we all, have carved-in family, peer group and particular community ways of acting. The remnants are not words, although my words can repeat my parents. This is not a text. I am marked with their actions – strips, slivers, gestures (action matter) – that I now reproduce, recut and perform. My action is woven with thread spun from their lives. My parents have left in me an aspect of their behavioural vocabulary. It is an imprint. Seeing it does not mean they are visible; it is an impression, a new version that is now exhibited through me. A shadow that casts an outline over my actions that does not have clear content. It is scattered barely connected fragments – matter. In the act of observing me, my family construct the shape of my father or my mother. It becomes visible only in the moment of interpreting action.

If you look very closely, the shadow itself turns out to be a mosaic. A multiple impression of many past fathers, mothers, sisters, friends and others. The action matter of 'new' moments is constructed from the tiniest embodied fragments of many others. These are Sheldon's 'little dramatic performances' but refracted through history. My father is thus marked in me and many were marked in and through him. We are as Scheurich writes 'webbed, arrayed, archaeological' and through however many layers we might dig, we will never find an original.

I rub my hands to create a friction and then clap them together. I do this whenever I am in a cold place, in a queue, or sitting in a traffic jam. I do it when I am just about to start something. It is my 'right, lets get this sorted' action. It has a verbal script and a predictable rhythm. It has a variety of cognitive justifications and creates an affective resonance in me. It is action but it is also a performance. It annoys people. This routine was my mother's. Is my mother's. I have flashes of memory where my mother would rub her hands together and irritate me as a child. Rub, rub, rub. Clap, clap, clap. At the end of the rubbing, several claps would indicate that now we should move on, get on with what we were doing, or that her impatience was growing. This is an action phrase – a mark that I have 'incorporated' and now perform. A simplistic analysis of my actions would condense them as evidence of me being a product of the behavioural flourishes of others. To a certain extent I am. I am constructed with the raw substance of what I have learnt and imitated. I remember, I think, copying it. However, now I rub my hands together without a conscious selection of the material. I do not only perform this, it is *my* behaviour. Therefore, its meaning cannot be found only in its origin, but in how I use it today. It is a 'piece' of action that although pretending to have a clear signifier (my mother's rubs and claps), now constructs its own set of meanings. It is evidence that I am a marked person, however I create my life with, through and not necessarily constricted by its possibilities. In the beginning there was reproduction 'everything begins with reproduction' (Derrida 1978, p. 211). In the beginning there was a training, a copying and only later did it become to rephrase Schechner, 'one with our body'. Once carved into us, we claim it as our own. We assume it is our 'behaviour'.

It is very hard to make a clear distinction, therefore, between reproduction and behaviour, or similarly between performance and behaviour. My actions are creations from a great variety of phrases, gestures, expressions and emotions. But they are reproductions, and in being reproductions, they will always be performances. Almost every action labelled 'behaviour' is constructed with reproduced action matter. We are not the *tabula rasa* onto which performance skills are written. All action is constructed and therefore there is no automatic temporal relation between behaviour and performance. One can come before the other, one can be in the other and one can come after the other. Applied theatre does not meet the neutralised bodies of its participants, but in creating theatre people are starting from and playing with the rich, dynamic and changing action matter that makes up their lives.

The baby-copying picture

Three pictures of a man and three of a baby (Sheldon, 1995, p. 100). First man-picture shows him poking out his tongue, second man-picture shows his mouth open wide and third man-picture shows his lips pursed. Underneath, first baby-picture poking out its tongue, second baby-picture mouth open wide and third baby-picture lips pursed.

These pictures are fascinating in many ways. They can be used to speak of origins, first actions and genetically determined behaviour. However I believe they simultaneously undermine any concept of originality. There are two performances shown – of the man and of the baby. The man is making shapes with his mouth, sticking out his tongue in order to elicit a response from the infant. He wants it to replicate his actions. He wants to cast a shadow on the child and for it to recreate an image of him. He enacts the deeply held but unobtainable desire vital to human reproduction. That is our hope that what we reproduce will be an image of ourselves. Reproduction in the biological sense is both an act of creation and re-creation. You aspire to leave a copy. Often the first comment of a person seeing a new baby will be a reference to the child's similarities with either the father or mother. One of the first actions a new father or mother will make, as is retold in this image, is to encourage the baby to further imitate them. 'She not only looks like me, she behaves like me.' The baby becomes the audience for parental performances. It is the sheet that they attempt to mark and vitally in the sense described by Scheurich, the body with which they seek to build interdependence. The image shows a man, gently and lovingly, marking the body of the baby and 'intermeshing' it within the lives of the parents.

The adults' behaviour is not guesswork. Why do they make these faces? They know something already. They push for a reaction and for imitation. The act of sticking out the tongue is an action learnt elsewhere. It is an action fragment dragged up and recreated for the 'new' experience. It can be understood as 'restored' or 'twice-behaved behavior' (Schechner, 2002, p. 23), even if it not the ritual practice that was originally defined by these terms.

The baby responds with 'simple imitation' (Sheldon, 1995, p 81). It is a copy: a rough, struggling and dribbling reinterpretation of the performance it sees before it, binding the baby to its audience. However, as with all copies, it is an imperfect version of the original (which in itself, was a version of some other). The baby is copying and performing a received action; one made of facial muscle formations, but once enacted it becomes part of the baby's bodily repertoire. Moving the muscles in this way will create associated sensations that thereafter will make this performance an action seemingly belonging to the infant. Exercising a muscle, however slightly, always changes that muscle. It is an action that will become part of the structure from which the infant can improvise. A structure that is forever intermeshed beyond its own body. 'Marking' is done on you; but once incorporated, the results become contours and capabilities that connect beyond you.

Experiments with what the psychologist Albert Bandura called 'lower-scale' animals showed that they can only repeat actions shown them concurrently or shortly afterwards (Bandura 1977, p. 38). The ability to repeat at some time later occurs higher up the animal scale. The baby in this picture is repeating concurrently. The link with the father requires at this stage the father's presence. However because the baby incorporates that 'rough dribbling' action through the repeated interaction with the parent, it will potentially be displayed and linked to the cooing and cajoling of other family members at other times. It is important to emphasise that this is not a competency stored mentally for future recall, but a shaping that becomes part of the physical and psychological potential of the person. The relationship between marking and future performance is of course central to assumptions within applied theatre. The action displayed by the father is not, nor can it be, faithfully produced by the infant. The rehearsal might mark, but the father cannot guarantee how those marks will be displayed. All of us will only ever produce 'rough, struggling, dribbling' reinterpretations of the performances we have witnessed. The important aspect here is not in the mark but in the nature of the link between that mark and the context. The way a person's performances are bound into a family, community and a wider social context – the strength of those complex webs – is one place where theatre-based projects can have their effect.

The baby-copying pictures hint that the greatest part of human action is the result of a complex history of imitations. The baby does not show us that it has some innate abilities for tongue sticking and mouth moving. It has an ability to take what it sees and copy it for an audience. The baby is thus committing an early act of performance. In copying, it always fails to create the perfect replica, but the copy works itself into the baby, to become part of the substance of potential future actions. The baby is constantly performing its daily learning life as a repeated action of building links with its context. This image is the opening lesson in playing with the 'matter of action'. The baby learns its first components, repeated concurrently for now; but gradually the marks become more detailed, and the ability to reproduce more sophisticated. The 'mesh' becomes more fixed and secure. The first deliberate actions we make are thus reproductions of others. These imperfect copies *become* residues, phrases, or gestures for exhibition and reworking later when there is a network that will accept, permit and give meaning to their execution. Our actions might appear as personal behaviour, but an archaeology reveals remnants of previous individuals' actions. Thus, performance is not only 'restored behavior' (Schechner, 1993, p. 1), but also 'behaviour' is a result of repeated performance.

Everybody will have copied the gestures of heroes, favourite villains, friends, relations, teachers and others. Actions often reveal a hidden aspiration to be a perfect copy of a perceived ideal. However, this is made difficult by the fact that you can never recreate the whole role. A person may know that she or he is a pale imitation of an idol, but she or he will continue to strive to be like that admired other. At the same time however people create themselves as examples of their difference. They often try desperately to be unlike certain figures in their pasts, but rarely succeed fully. You find echoes, phrases and actions re-emerging when they are least expected. Whether you try to 'do as well as others' or 'not do as your parents did', all behaviour has impressed into its skin that it is still a copy.

From behaviour to performance?

Yes, but also from performance to behaviour. Imitation leads to action as action can lead to imitation. In any action, multiple elements are displayed. Recent imitations and past observations. The reworking of a gait observed here and a gesture witnessed there. A repeated version that has become so secure that it is physically part of a repertoire with unfathomable origin. We display copies, extracts, and chunks of behaviour that because all copies have an ambiguous relation to an original, can appear original in themselves. As I commented in the introduction, 'behaviour' is often considered as generating from the self outwards, forgetting that it too is constructed; it is a series of marks. We should seek therefore to avoid definitions that produce a hierarchical relationship of origins between behaviour and performance. Performance can be 'behavior heightened' (Schechner, 1993, p. 1), indicating that it is a transformed version of other behaviours. However, behaviour can also be defined as incorporated performance, coming after the reproduction as witnessed in the baby picture. This latter definition insists that there was no Adam baby who first stuck out his tongue. We are all Eves. As Schechner writes 'there is no such thing as "once-behaved behavior"' (Schechner, 2002, p. 23). This is not to deny any temporal shift in actions and how they are displayed, because there is a movement from an action being imitated immediately to it becoming a flourish that is used with ease. This process shifts from simply displaying other's actions to showing the marks of those actions on and through one's own body. This is related to the Kathakali training but here I am using it to explain a much more gradual process of learning in the everyday. It resembles the move from writing by copying the letters of your teacher to writing. Existing within the constructions that are called 'behaviours' and the most elaborate performances are a rich array of action fragments. Within one performance there may be a reiteration of many previous actions. Within one 'behaviour' several marks will be revealed and may be witnessed. My hand rubbing is a performance and a 'behaviour' – it is an action. I rub my hands without explicitly imagining it as a repetition of my mother. It is now 'action matter' that is free from its signifier and creates its own dynamics and possible meanings. There is a temporal distance from when I first made this action and how I perform it today, however this does not demonstrate a simple move from behaviour to performance.

The matter of action

Action – a marking of and a marking from the body. Our action is a series of received 'bits of behaviour', mediated cognitive/affective responses, learnt scripts, tried and tested shrugs, practised movements, hardwired outbursts and controlled performances. These are its raw materials; the marks, utterances and substance of the moving body. We create our lives with this matter and become ourselves as we do so. However, by becoming ourselves we construct a (hi)story, and that experience becomes a new fragment: a new mark on our body. It offers material from which to enact the next moment. Personal repertoires become displayed as actions in the social world, and actions become fresh memory or marking processes. We may become ourselves as we act, but we do so with a jumble of matter that is already produced. Theatre training, although of course including the spoken and written word, is vitally the deliberate and explicit process of playing with the 'matter of action'. A play or a scene in an improvisation can therefore reveal the hidden textures of our bodies as we perform as well as leaving traces on those bodies. A theatre performance is created with the marks of the body and creates new marks on the body. In so doing, it creates resources for future performances. This minute and complex interaction with the carved-in-action memories provides the place from which the explicit use of theatre techniques with the non-theatre practitioner can find its power. This does not insist that applied theatre should be the lengthy process of actor training, but an engagement with the marked and interconnected actions of participants. Even the shortest applied-theatre project can adjust the links between people and enact new relations between groups that rub against and reveal the marks of our lives.

Marking

Rituals often include the marking of the body. Scarring and circumcision, for example, literally cut the flesh. They mark and make a distinction bodily. This external mark, however, is often a symbol of the process of internal marking. Ritual can 'mark' and thus make the change from adolescence to adulthood. The act of performance, (repeating the observed actions of others for an actual or anticipated audience) also marks the body. It develops muscle structure, limb flexibility, affective states, new cognitive processes and thought patterns (the 'body' here of course includes the mind/brain). An extreme and arguably brutal form of this is seen in the Kathakali training described by Schechner. Here however, I am using the word 'mark' to explain a less rigorous process where gradual adjustments to our 'action matter' occur through learning and imitating behaviour at every moment in our lives. This can be in obvious moments of role play but also in the smallest incidents of the everyday. For example, the marching of the soldier makes patterns in that person's body. The forced out chest of the sergeant is a vivid and visible mark. It is the evidence of a 'body already hardened by habit into a certain set of actions and reactions' (Boal, 1992, p. 40). However, marking can also be the subtler process of a person practising their smile in a mirror, learning to click their fingers or a child adjusting their accent to a new school. You can be an object of the process, but also – vitally for applied theatre – subject of it. For example, a child can choose to repeat the walk of a favoured teacher, wink like a particular idol or restate the words of an admired sister. In playing with these actions, you mark yourself very slightly, ensuring that your next action will be negotiated through that structure. You can use the potential you already have adaptively and act to recreate yourself for new experiences.

People, however, can also be marked by the conduct of others. Repeated acts of love or cruelty will leave action fragments that shape the way person engages (intermeshes) with incidents in their future. Oppression, violence, bullying or exclusion all act to mark and mesh a person within certain structures of action. New situations will be negotiated through the shapes of that history, revealing those previous marking moments and giving the contours for present-day inter-actions. The sergeant's chest can be the pattern through which his current responses will be formed, leaving an impression beyond the context in which it was originally created. Different experiences will fit into the creases of your past or form new lines above them. Actions are constructed with and through a history, creating fresh marks in the present. An event could deepen that line or create new shapes on which different actions could be built. A mark can be so deep that it will be always raw and heavily accent any future actions. One event however will never create a predicable mark in others, because it necessarily reacts to the particular shape of the person it meets. Oppression will never have a single effect, and can leave marks prompting both submission and resistance.

An applied-theatre workshop programme can act to subtly reveal the marks carried through the bodies of participants and simul-taneously offer a powerful set of experiences that provide a positive, marking moment. In playing with roles, scripts and stories, you can develop a fluency in the possibilities of your own body and connect that body to new groups or communities. In this process, new configurations emerge that themselves will leave traces – gestures, shrugs, smiles, verbal quips, frowns and hand movements – from which future interactions may be constructed. This does not start from the erased body of the Kathakali dancer, but is directed by the richly shaped, embodied experience of the participant. The strength of this process depends on the length and the context of the project. However, even the shortest theatre workshop, much like the single and simple act of the father sticking out his tongue, can leave networks between people, creating new minute linked action fragments that can compete, constrict or lie above hurtful marks from the past.

The cognitive God

Performances are encoded into particular image sequences and word symbols and stored into memory. (Sheldon, 1995, p. 85)

Whereas the process of turning performances into sequences and symbols is connected to the idea that action is constructed from multiple embodied fragments, the expression here demands an interim coder. This encoding implies a governing subject: an organiser, filer and arranger. It implies a memory-retrieval system that is not in itself a construct of a history of actions or performances. Encoding should perhaps more usefully be reframed as the process of marking that I am discussing here. Rather than a neat organisational code, the experience of action, through repetitions and observations, has become carved into our bodies (and clearly, as stated previously, there is no division here between the brain and the body). They are not decoded in order to be performed, rather they are the structure through which we act, the shape of which can facilitate or restrict depending on the circumstance. Observations are burnt into the back of our retina and we see through this frame. Sounds form our inner ear and we hear through its shape. Actions imprint themselves in our muscles, and we push and pull with their strength or flexibility. The way I rub my hands together vigorously to keep warm is a mark from my mother. However, there is no longer an in-between code which I somehow decode in order to repeat her hand rubbing. It is a repeat, but now it is in me and I perform it as part of my own body.

In the quotation above, the mediation that is required for decoding and coding is handed over to powerful 'cognition'. To restate the opening quote, it 'allows us to re-enact, in symbolic form, the little dramatic performances we have selected from the behaviour of others' (Sheldon, 1995, p. 86). Cognition is viewed as the process of scripting and rescripting the source materials. The 'little dramatic performances' are maintained but then chopped into a variety of sections. Sheldon calls these a 'mental script' (Sheldon, 1995, p. 86) but I am uncomfortable with the 'completeness' of this metaphor. The word 'script' implies the whole play, whole characters or whole roles.

Our resources are not whole but disparate fragments of minute actions that we pull together as we act. Some coalesce around certain moments of dialogue, specific scenarios, or well-known roles but they are rarely complete. The richer a person's experiences, the more varied the sources of these fragments, the greater flexibility and apparent spontaneity there will be in performance. Repeated single routines will lead to an impoverished regurgitation of large performance chunks, stereotypical and obvious. They will cut deep lines that will produce a familiar contour to numerous different social acts. Again, applied theatre plays with the notion of flexibility in performance by providing new physical routines (in games and exercises), new action resources (the acting of unfamiliar characters in new locations) and the experience of chopping and reworking a range of action matter (through participation in theatrical rehearsal, improvisation or performance). This is then a heightened, explicit and concentrated version of what continues in people's daily lives. The ability to play and create with a multitude of actions is as important as the need for those actions to be extended and new marking moments to be experienced. As I say above, if the cut is repeated frequently, the mark becomes deeper and more permanent. A person with long-term experience of recurrent painful 'little dramatic performances' will struggle not to have this affect their daily actions. Applied-theatre programmes cannot compete with the vividness of these marks, but can engage groups and communities in revealing and acknowledging the action matter of their lives. In that process they create the tiniest marks that can build fragile structures laced over the old. These do not deny the marks of the past, but set up the possibility for new shapes through which a person many negotiate their future.

This argument seeks to question the whole notion of mediation. It rejects the implication that there is somehow a great and powerful decoder or scriptor. The model should be more fluid as espoused by the philosopher D. C. Dennet, when he rejects a 'Cognitive God':

> There is no central Headquarters, no Cartesian theatre where 'it all comes together' for the perusal of a Central Meaner. Instead of such a single stream (however wide) there are multiple channels in which specialist circuits try, in

parallel pandemoniums to do their various things, creating Multiple Drafts as they go. (Dennet, 1991, p. 63, quoted in Sheldon, 1995, p. 38)

These channels are the lines of marks that I have been discussing here, but importantly they link 'beyond the brain' to the interdependent consciousness argued for by Scheurich. The 'multiple drafts' for action (although I do not like the textual metaphor) are created within and crucially between people. The channels do not exist only as unique archaeology of the individual but are linked, interwoven and often shared between groups.

This said, the Cognitive God is not abolished so easily. It appeared in Bandura's work when he argued that 'during exposure observers acquire mainly symbolic representations of the modelled activities which serve as guides for appropriate performances' (Bandura, 1977, p. 24). He is stating that during the process of observational learning and subsequent performance, the series of codes 'serve as' guides to our behaviour. Again, this presupposes an ordering, decoding and sorting 'Meaning Maker', who seeks to edit behaviour cleanly and place it in a correct context – the mediator I speak of above. The guide is somehow fixed or fixable. The process of behaving has a cognitive guardian who coolly chooses the 'appropriate performance'. As I have already stated, we need to question the existence of guides/gods. Instead, it should be emphasised that the 'code' is permanently growing, shifting, changing and adapting. It is matter, not a text or a book. We have multiple action fragments imprinted mentally and corporeally. These also exist within and between individuals. The 'store' – (Dennet's 'channels') does not have fixed boundaries, neat walls and a comprehensive filing or retrieval system. The store too is a moving constructed set of shapes. It is part of a 'pandemonium' rather than order. If our observation of others' action is coded as a guide, a rational process of using guides must be engaged in. We find the answer in the book. The emphasis on the rational interpretation and implementation of a coded structure of behaviour should be countered with an alternative view that rejects books of codes as a false 'natural totality' (Derrida, 1974, p. 30). The creative process should not separate cognition as a distinct and free-floating moment. Some type of selection happens but what makes one word appear, one phrase be uttered and one action performed cannot be reduced to a powerful decoder in the head. Words/phrases/actions are reproduced through a minute interweaving between all different codes/channels in the body. In the specific act of writing these words, these extend from the ligaments in my typing fingers to the synapses in my brain.

Cognition is also a mark, a structure of memories, past events, spoken words and narratives. Nothing sits beyond all these things and sorts them. Cognition can rehearse but it has structured limitations to how it rehearses. We might think and plan before acting, but visible behaviour is created in the actual. The preplanning has no automatic, complete or purely representational relation to the future event. It does not embody behaviour.

Stealing

However original we believe our actions to be they are still 'stolen behaviour'. Action matter 'is never specific to its author or its recipient' (Derrida, 1978, pp. 264–6). Our actions are our own, but they are also the property of others.

> A child who watches others breaking down a fence with consummate skill need not perform similar behaviour on the next fence he comes across. A variety of different conditions [...] some of them social in origin, will determine when the behaviour 're-emerges'. In the meantime, aspects of the performance are represented in memory waiting to be called up for future circumstances. (Sheldon, 1995, p. 83)

According to this perspective, therefore, the child in breaking down a fence in the future will be demonstrating the re-emergence of this behaviour. S/he has stolen it and coded it; and it will come butterfly-like from its cocoon. The precise meaning of this 're-emergence' is unclear. Again, it seems to imply a rational decoding of neat chunks of experience. More accurately, I would argue that it should be conceived of as a fluid process. Breaking down a fence is an affective

66

trace and a mark in the child. It will not re-emerge in its complete form, or be revealed precisely in a future fence-breaking incident. Whatever happens, it will be a new embodiment of this action. It will no longer be it; it will be part of something else. No fence will be broken in the exactly the same way. Maybe the strike of the fist against the wood will find its way to a playground incident. Maybe the cheers when the fence came down will be reworked through a fight with a sibling. Maybe the kicking of the panels will be visible in the kicking of cans in the street. The observed incident, rather than being faithfully replayed, is as likely to be barely recognisable in the future action of the young person. Whereas any later action will not belong to the child – it is stolen – he or she now creates new sets of meanings from it. It will 'intermesh' with other people and other environments, without obvious or explicit connections with its past.

Applied theatre is stealing. It takes the process of theatre into new contexts and constructs a confused set of meanings from it. In doing so, it does not leave in participants a performance skill to be simply replayed later. Rehearsal does not leave a role to be reformed but a series of possible action fragments that might appear as an accent or echo in a real moment some time in the future. Reading those moments will reveal a multiple and complex theft of action matter. However, as in all performances, it will be hard to trace the owners. The impact of theatre workshops, performances, role playing or drama games cannot be understood as training of the decoder or providing collections of replicable skills. They work, extend and transform the channels of experience that lie within and between people – perhaps multiplying the 'multiple drafts', and more often boosting the healthy pandemonium that is the real stimulus for human action.

Adolescence

Modelling is the process through which we learn the speech patterns of our parents and peers; learn to act like our favourite film star; pick up the rudiments of a new dance style; learn how to behave in strange surroundings; how to approach strangers for amorous purposes; how to imitate others; come to approach decision-making in as neurotic a way as our parents; learn how being aggressive gets people their way, or not. (Sheldon, 1995, p. 81)

During adolescence we seek models and copy them. We experiment with different styles of behaviour in order to create 'distinct' identity. As we experiment, we create ourselves using fragments of action: the resources of action matter. Comfort with this shifting self 'is only achieved later when judicious editing, fluency and the combining of different performances produces a genuinely unique style of behaviour' (Sheldon, 1995, p. 81). Here Sheldon uses terminology from both writing (editing) and speech (fluency), implying that 'behaviour' is structured like a text. While I believe that the two-dimensional precision of the 'text' metaphor misses the complexity of the embodied 'pandemonium' of action, it does recognise the constructed nature of human 'behaviour'. However, I also believe that Sheldon is mistaken in stating that a 'unique' behaviour is created at the end of this process. It is neither unique nor not unique – it is simultaneously stolen and original. Young people are in a shifting and often fraught state of developing performance skills. They are frequently trying to distance themselves from one set of actions (perhaps those of their parents) while displaying, with acute attention to detail, the correct behaviour for their peer group. This is a developing competence, with some young people performing crude versions of multiple influences, and with others demonstrating fabulously creative and interpretative power. Theatre programmes working with adolescents are thus an intervention in an ongoing performance development process. They are no more likely to create pure role models (through characterisation) than the experiential marking moments that young people are already meeting. What they can provide are new interactions that positively carve new channels within and between young people. They offer a staging post between the modelling and the improvisation where the matter of action can be played with freely.

Memories

Sometimes we think about the reasons for our behaviour *as* we behave. At other times stimuli give rise to memories, thoughts and feelings about potential actions which we perform later. (Sheldon, 1995, p. 68)

The structure of these memories becomes relevant because they are part of our action resources. They are however both individual and communal. They are, to paraphrase Scheurich, intermeshed with their context. As I have already stated when discussing the channels or marks created by action, it is vital to conceive of them as going beyond the boundary of the individual. They are in fact part of the web that links and connects with other people or groups. The shape of an experience can be revealed and then aligned with the form of another. Mutual understanding can be forged through common action histories or surprising links can be created between very different people. This process is what transforms personal experiences into bonds between groups. Some aspects of behaviour become components of culture when they are held in common within families, peer groups, communities or historical periods. Removing a person from a situation, through migration, imprisonment, expulsion or many other forms of dislocation, can tear the connections in the web that holds a person in place. A person content with their position will have marks that are welded strongly between them and their community. When taken from that situation, a person acts desperately to re-discover or reform connections that can make his or her own actions meaningful. This dislocation and subsequent fraying of the web, is the bewilderment discussed in the introduction and is taken up as a major theme in the next chapter where the focus is the transition from prison back to the community.

Memory that results in action is partly individual; but when it is held communally, it becomes the basis of tradition. That might be small family traditional actions (for example a particular way of celebrating anniversaries) or wider social traditions (such as annual festivals or religious events). This is significant for applied theatre because these events involve the creation of common experiences between groups which are realised through different performance forms, and are vital for a community's sense of identity and well-being. They are crucial in creating or maintaining the 'webs of significance' that make up a particular culture (Geertz, 1973, p. 5). Rather than being the daily use of action matter, applied-theatre projects attempt to replicate the power of these events through the deliberate playing with action fragments. This intentional, planned activity means that groups can develop a powerful awareness of the structure of their lives, and vitally create memories that are shared between participants. There is intensity to this process. It involves amongst other activities, energetic play, the group recreation of small incidents, the rehearsal of more complex scenes and the display of these in performance. There is a heat or energy created by the organisation of the theatre project that increases the degree of its impact. The collective activity creates a force that binds people and forms the bonds that are the substance of Scheurich's mesh or web. This structure then supports people and gives them memories that are held in common. Every moment of performance, and particularly the public acts or displays of a group's theatrical work, actively creates the 'webs of significance' between people. The experience can be a form of 'social energy' (see Uphoff, 1996, p. 357 and chapter two) that allows certain connections to be melted, and new ones to be formed. Fresh marks are made, are forged, by the strength of the activity and thereafter become incorporated memories that exist as a resource for individual and community action. These might be slight, imperceptible or minor in comparison with the deep structure of our lives, but they are made and held all the same. Applied theatre in creating activities based on developing confidence in the use of action matter is a process that can link and bind groups through common experience. These can then become memories revealed at another time. However crucially, while acknowledging the orientation to the future, applied theatre is an activity that in creating these marks and forming those connections, is a process that makes those changes in the present.

Why can't they see the view?

Between the age of 13 and 16 I spent every summer in Edinburgh, working in various theatres. In my mid-twenties, I returned to the city and discovered that it was beautiful: in my mind, the most eye-catching city in Britain.

In 1997, I visited the Grand Canyon with my partner and two daughters aged four and six. While we adults admired what we could see, my two girls played in the dirt piling pebbles on top of each other with their backs to the view.

In a car on a family journey, my eldest daughter once said, 'I spy with my little eye something beginning with 'V' – 'Verge', guessed my wife. – 'Vest', I tried. 'No', she continued, 'it is something that Mummy always sees and always likes'. We gave up – 'View', she proclaimed, triumphantly.

Children cannot see and they struggle with the concept of 'views'. Adolescents are learning to see them. I am not sure at what age finally your eyes can perceive distance in a way that allows you to reflect and make judgements upon it, but my contention here is that the ability to find pleasure in a 'view' is linked to reflective skills generally, and an important aspect of understanding action and performance. Perception of distance develops and is not automatic. Similarly perspective taking or understanding the impact of action, is learnt and practised. This is part of the same pattern that moves from the baby repeating concurrently, to repeating some time after the first moment. Gradually being able to draw upon a wide range of action fragments, long since disconnected from when and where they were originally encountered, is a developed ability. The closeness that children have to the experiences that mark them, makes them perceive from a limited set of reference points. The views are still new, and are processed for what they are (trees, mountains, rivers), not for how they compare to the imprinted memories of others.

A lack of developed perception is widely understood as central to the problems faced by certain groups of adolescents. Young people with 'problem behaviour' are identified as having poor perspective-

71

taking skills (see Rose, 1998; Chandler, 1973). This problem becomes the focus for interventions that aim to make these young people 'act' in a different way. Their current actions (whether these are offending, rule-breaking in school – or other activities that cause concern) demonstrate that they struggle to see beyond the moment. They find it hard to problem-solve effectively or anticipate the consequences of their actions. Of course this is not only a skill lacking in so-called delinquents. This inability to reflect and see beyond the moment, although affecting behavioural decisions in adolescence, is, as I claim above, directly linked to a failure to appreciate the panoramic. 'View' is therefore both a spatial and a temporal concept in the development of potential and skill. My children had neither spatial nor temporal in/sight.

Much therapeutic work with troubled young people seeks to develop their perspective-taking abilities. Many applied-theatre processes explicitly seek to teach people to examine the consequences of their actions. In these projects, a person is warned that 'if you do x, y might happen'. Think before you act. Look before you leap. Narrative-based workshops – or educational plays – will explore consequences, futures, plot lines and the links between cause and effect. This work fails in one sense. It assumes that the 'view seeing' is already in place and that the young people are simply looking in the wrong direction. The play stands them in front of the view and they are told to look. They are impressed with the consequences of the actions, and asked to understand. They are given, for example, a vision of a death by 'joyriding' and expected not to steal cars. However, no amount of standing in Edinburgh castle and looking over ramparts would have made me see the beauty of the town when I was a teenager. The view was there ('I spy with my little eye something beginning with V') but there was no set of resources through which a reflection could take place.

We need therefore, over time, to learn to look, not be told what to look at. The ability needs to be encouraged, and experiences offered that provide possible resources that can inspire perception. Theatre programmes that rely on showing narratives based on the consequences of decisions are thus in danger of doing the equivalent of presenting views and asking people to look. They can easily forget that reflection needs a set of experiences against which judgements can be made. Perception, view watching, requires a series of marks, memories and action fragments that should be developed without simply insisting that they are skills that are automatically held. The learning needs to happen before the objects for our attention are presented. It should not be 'don't do this because that will happen'. Young people are in a state of learning gradually to look back, forward and into the distance. Their behaviour can move from simple copying to bad reproductions, to sophisticated reworkings. There is no point in dragging them to the beautiful view, pointing and expecting them to understand your awe.

Participating in theatre

If action and interaction both perform a complex reworking of previous fragments, and at the same time re-mark and create new affective imprints on the body – what happens when we participate in a theatre project? If those marks can connect between people creating a 'broader social or cultural or contextual field' – what impact can we claim for an applied-theatre process? These questions have been touched on above, but I want to conclude by exploring them further. Role play, theatre workshops, participation in theatre games or watching a performance are all actions which interact in a complex way with our existing embodied histories, and bring us into contact with particular networks of human activity. It would be wrong to say that we pick up skills, attitudes or roles from these experiences and display them later. I have argued throughout this chapter that action is not mechanistically (re)created this way. However, theatre, in being an explicit play with and around 'action matter', deals with the basic processes of how we learn to perform our lives. Actions undertaken or witnessed in theatre will leave emotional memories, behaviour fragments, characteristics, lines, gestures and images of self that will fit or conflict with an existing shape. In fitting, they become part of the material that can be recreated, reworked and displayed in later life: not as a simple reproduction at the correct moment, but as a resource that will be implicit in the engagements we make with the world. In conflicting, they might be discarded; but even in that dismissal the structure of an action will have been changed through the emphatic act of rejection. In every event the matter of action is shared, connected and intermeshed with that of others. So, for example, the heightened pleasure of applause might leave an imprint of pride that will be both accidentally and explicitly performed in future actions. It could be a feeling that is flashed through interactions in a huge variety of situations but it will be replayed as pride only when a future context permits that meaning to be realised. The energy of theatre games could instil a confidence that will be seen in a person's comfort in working with others. However, if there is no place for it to be displayed, the mark of confidence will not be revealed. A line repeated in a scene may be said in the dinner queue, but the effect will be new. The attitude of a character being played by a child in a school play may surface in a mealtime interaction with a parent, perhaps inadvertently but occasionally deliberately performed. The mark of that attitude will only be visible and understandable in the way it produces a contour beyond the body into the context of that new interaction.

However, in playing with multiple fragments of action, theatre processes are not only creating potential future re-enactments, they are also working in the actual. They carve and join people in real moments that change as they happen, and not only in the diversity of action fragments that they might leave for the future. Connections – those webs – are formed and reformed in the live moment of a theatre performance, workshop or rehearsal. These are links that could be strengthened by new experiences because once created a mesh will linger and reconnect with a similar not necessarily identical other. However, they could also, once the event is over, gradually dissolve to the point that connecting with other even slightly similar experiences is difficult or even impossible. Theatre transforms, but there is nothing inevitable about the future result of those transformations.

Scratching at the surface of each of us, we need to find more than the one character or one event replaying itself through our lives. We want to be the rich result of fathers, mothers, sisters, brothers, friends, teachers, artists, writers and others. However, sometimes those markers have left deep scars that reveal themselves in troubled, hurtful or oppressive actions. These then bind us to communities or networks that secure a meaning for that history but maintain the depth of the grooves. These communities can maintain, enhance and justify certain behaviours that in many ways we hope to avoid or leave behind. By participating in a diverse set of theatre-based activities, our bodies can experience actions that avoid the narrow, stereotypical, and singular. We can perhaps reconnect, attach or weave ourselves into a range of groups or communities. We can perhaps strengthen our ability to display actions that build new webs that can provide some of the foundation for change.

And we want to use these inspiring resources to see as much of the view as possible.

Chapter Two
Theatre in bewilderment

This chapter takes up some of the theoretical issues raised in chapter one to explore the history of employment-training programmes for prisoners and three particular examples of theatre-based practice in this field. It is the first of four chapters in the book that aim to apply some of the schema already outlined to specific examples of applied-theatre work. In discussing projects and issues through this framework it is hoped that the potential of this way of approaching applied theatre will be further illustrated. Each chapter does not strictly explore one aspect of the theory, however. It prioritises an area of practice, using aspects or developing parts of the approach to discover more about that work. At times, the chapters will introduce further theoretical terms that aid the examination of the particular example that they seek to debate. These will, I hope, augment the outline in chapter one, making the theoretical premise develop as the book unfolds.

This chapter concentrates on examples of prison employment-training programmes, and in particular prison theatre projects that have employment-related themes. As I stated in the introduction, prison is where my applied-theatre work was first developed, and it seems appropriate, therefore, that it is from here that the analysis in this book starts. I have also discussed how applied theatre cannot be relegated only to an analysis of the moments of the theatre workshop or performance. The meetings, advocacy, and the research into the context must also be part of 'practising applied theatre'. For this reason this chapter both analyses theatre projects with a particular purpose in the prison system, and also explores the logic of an aspect of that system using theatrical terms and concepts. I am analysing applied theatre and applying theatre in my analysis.

Employment projects in prison belong to a particular moment in the developing discourse on prison rehabilitation. As this chapter hopes to demonstrate, this debate is part of a shifting history of theories about criminal-justice interventions. The interest in employment developed from the particular emphasis on the employability of ex-offenders that was prevalent in the final years of John Major's Conservative government (1992–7) and was restated by the Labour party's interest in 'New Start' initiatives for a range of long-term unemployed communities. This position was very strong at the beginning of the New Labour administration (1997), and while still apparent in 2002, it is already losing its significance. The recent emphasis on 'key skills' and basic educational needs has led to a move away from this earlier priority of securing the ex-prisoner's 'employability'. Of course, educational attainment is linked to employment, but these two areas are also competing concerns within the political debates in the government. Employment projects in prison in 1997 were thus an example of the strength of that area within these debates, not the evidence that these approaches were timeless answers to prisoners' problems. These shifts remind us that at each moment of theatre application we are entering an arena where 'current' practice is no more than a historically and culturally specific result of different social, political and ideological interests. This chapter is thus discussing an intervention that is wedded to a moment in the frequent changes in criminal-justice thinking and practice. Applied-theatre practitioners created projects within that moment, in the same way that the recent publication 'Getting Our Act Together: a manual for the delivery of key skills and basic skills through drama' (UAOP Publications, 2002) is a specific response to the particular context of this new time. The problems that emerge when theatre practitioners enter an arena without a conscious recognition of the specificity of the practice that they meet provide important lessons for the field. Applied theatre's ability to recreate itself for a context, in comparison to its need to maintain clarity of principle and intent, is therefore a 'balancing act' that is touched upon in this chapter and will be returned to later in the book.

Bewilderment

> An overdose of sensory perception [...] its very strange. (Prisoner discussing experience of leaving prison in Simon, 1999, p. 163)

Although I have already outlined a definition of bewilderment, Simon uses it in a criminal-justice context (Simon, 1999, p. 163) to explain specifically the confused or perplexed state that many prisoners have reported they find themselves in on leaving prison. It relates to problems of adjustment and the dissonance caused by the differing expectations and experiences of prison and the outside world. Into this area of bewilderment come the hopes of professionals who want to smooth the transition and ease prisoners back into society. Over time attempts at supporting prisoners in this move have included programmes of religious conversion, psychological intervention, hard labour, education and, in the case discussed here, employment-training projects. Prison for some governors, probation officers and criminal justice commentators has been understood at certain moments as the rehearsal site for life outside. A place where men and women can learn skills, habits and attitudes that can be enacted back in free society. For others, however, this is a flawed vision. These alternative readings claim prison can never be this rehearsal and must always be a separate unconnected 'real' space. The debate between these two positions can be seen in much of the discourse on prison rehabilitation and reform. It is into this debate that this chapter places itself, specifically to doubt and question the promise of rehearsal and skills training. The previous chapter argued that there is no automatic link between competencies learnt in one place and the likelihood of future display in another. This analysis will now be used in a context that has historically seen shifts in the debate between these arguments. The chapter will therefore explore how the situated, interrelated and constructed understanding of human action proposed in chapter one interacts with these discourses. It perhaps helps us to comprehend applied-theatre projects that of necessity are negotiating their practice within them.

The chapter starts with an overview of the history of prison work programmes seen through the lens of this discussion and continues by examining two projects by the Theatre in Prisons and Probation (TIPP) Centre in Manchester concerning employment. These projects deliberately took 'rehearsal' into spaces whose function was contested around this concept. Finally, the chapter will explore an initiative in the north-west of England which was created to 'bring community influence to the design of a prison regime and to provide a geographical, social and economic link between the prisoner and the environment to which he [sic] will return' (Lateral Associates, 1999, p. 3). The move to demanding 'community influence' represents another turn to which applied-theatre practitioners have sought to develop a response.

Some history

In offering an overview of the history of the way prisons have or have not prepared prisoners for employment on release, there are two caveats that must be mentioned because they vitally impact on the whole analysis. First, the historical examples of prison regimes and prison services that are under discussion no longer exist. This is stating the obvious but what it means is that I will be using descriptions and representations of those practices; and, as emphasised by the performance theorist Peggy Phelan, 'as a rep-resentation of the real the image is always partially phantasmic' (Phelan, 1993, p. 1). The link between the commentator's words and what they describe is ambiguous at best, and the words themselves cannot be divorced from the environments in which they functioned. This is as true of the documents of Lateral Associates mentioned above as it is of the descriptions from the eighteenth century. Frances Simon notes that in the time of John Howard in the 1770s the 'themes' in relation to writings on prison regimes were 'solitary confinement (in clean conditions), religion and hard work' (Simon, 1999, p. 2). These, however, were themes of writing; they functioned as rhetorical devices used by Howard in his advocacy of prison reform perhaps more than they described prisons. Although it is always impossible to separate analysis of practice from the rhetorical power of the analysis construction, these distinctions are acute in criminal-justice writing. Prisons and punishment have deep symbolic resonance in a number of cultural and historical contexts. The institutions, the practices within them and the writings on them, all exist in complex networks of symbol, signification and actuality and this system of ambiguity therefore mediates the whole of this chapter. Applied theatre meets these systems and negotiates its projects within the ambiguity of these moments, but is also easily beguiled by the comparative clarity of one specific practice or perspective. That beguilement of course has been touched upon in the introduction in the comments on the ease with which we slipped into advocating the cognitive behavioural account of prisoner rehabilitation. Here the 'tempting' arena was 'employment training programmes for young offenders'.

The second caveat is that in this historical overview I am applying performance concepts in the analysis of a social process. I am seeing this history through a very particular frame or lens (Grady, 1996, p. 60). I am not a prison-work programme expert but an applied-theatre analyst who is seeing this field from this perspective. As noted previously, my visitor status must be acknowledged. As an outsider to this discipline, I do not place theatrical metaphors onto the material, rather they emerge in the processes that are analysed. This is of course one very partial way of understanding these programmes. The application is deliberate (like a person tuning a radio to pick up a certain signal) and it is accidental (like a person responding allergically to microbes others might not feel). Applying theatre in an analysis of social phenomena – reading them 'as' performance – means that they are subjectively responded to and then constructed as performance processes. I would of course note that all commentators have different sensibilities/tunings/allergies through which they construct narratives. The one presented here is an explicitly performance-based one: deliberate and in the open.

To analyse the shifting rhetoric of prison work I am going to borrow terms taken from theories of language and used widely in performance theory (see Schechner, 2002, pp. 110–14). I will use 'constative', 'performative' and the invented word 'futuritive' to compare alternative descriptions of prison work. In Austin's (1962) original formulation, the constative and performative helped distinguish between speech that described (constative) and speech that enacted or did something (performative). The utterance 'I name this ship Elizabeth' was thus performative because it was an action. It named the ship as it was said. Rather than use these terms in a discussion of speech however, I will use all three to designate alternative explanations of prison work. The word 'futuritive' is created to explain prison programmes that are not done for their value in the present, but are enacted for the promise of what they should achieve. The futuritive projects are thus those that focus on rehearsal of skills or attitudes for the future. Work programmes that function as a 'statement' – projects that are done in the present without a direct concern for what they do are labelled 'constative'. They describe a state and are often there to occupy time. Work programmes that are done in order to have an effect at the moment of execution will be referred to as 'performative'. As they are implemented, an action – a change – is completed. It is clear that many projects may lay claim to one model but in their operation enact a different one. These terms therefore do not necessarily describe separate projects, but a single project can have constative, performative or futuritive elements.

Although punishment generally has often centred on the body of the prisoner as the site of performative interventions (see Garland, 1990; Foucault, 1977) prison work projects in particular have been described primarily as either constative or futuritive in their outlook. In certain periods, they were explained 'constatively'. Prison work was for the moment only, done to use time. In others the futuritive prevailed and prison work programmes were deemed to have a purpose that went beyond the immediate and acted as a preparation or a rehearsal for the future. In the early history of prisons the constative predominated, in later years it has been the futuritive that has been the principal preoccupation of prison service managers and policy makers. However, it would be false to see the development of prison programmes simply as a gradual move from the one to the other. They have always coexisted, collided and shifted in their relative importance. At the same moment, a particular commentator could emphasise one while another might be extolling the virtues of the other. They are turns in a moving and ongoing discursive debate.

Two of the earliest and most influential British commentators on the prison system were John Howard and Jeremy Bentham. Howard was perhaps the first recorded advocate of prison reform. He describes in the 1770s 'hard work' as something that was done, not necessarily what it was done for. For him prisons were arranged around the trinity of work, religion and solitude. Bentham on the other hand is famous for his panopticon design for prisons that he proposed from 1791. Its purpose was to create a profitable factory with self-disciplined workers where from a single vantage point the whole prison could be observed. Work was for profit and in no way related to a preparation for the prisoners. Both of these formulations seemed to support work in prisons as symbolically connected to penitence and godliness, but neither was concerned with the link between the moment in the prison and the free life of the prisoner. Prisons concentrated more on punishment in the now and a preparation for release of the prisoners into heaven rather than back in to the community. Although it could be argued that these approaches were performative because they were actions that inevitably affected the bodies of the prisoners, I am framing them as constative here because the emphasis was on a statement of containment. 'Hard work' was explained for what it was, not for what it sought to do.

After 1877, the first chair of the prison commissioners, Du Cane, made explicit a new purpose for prison work. His view was that labour could 'instil good work habits and knowledge of honest trades' (Simon, 1999, p. 4). This is echoed by the later Prison Commission annual report (1906–7) which stated that prison work 'may not directly lead to [...] employment in that particular trade on discharge, [but] will at least, give [...] the habit of applied labour' (Simon, 1999, p. 5). Between these two moments the 1877 Prison Act had centralised the prison system and made clear that work was only there as deterrence and punishment. Without forgetting that deterrence is always performed with the wider public audience in mind, the ideas of Du Cane and the Prison Commission hint at a shift to work being framed as futuritive. It is now part of a learning process. As an unsubtle form of behavioural therapy, repeated work was done in order to create 'habit'. There is a performative emphasis because the prison work enacts (it seeks to 'instil'), but this moves towards a concern for the future rather than an interest in the present. The skills are irrelevant, but repetition was viewed as way of moulding a character. This is linked to prison work as rehearsal, a preparation for something other, but is tied with a limited notion that work has some essential trait that will pass from one form of the activity to another. The assumption is that by owning that trait you can freely apply it to future work. As is outlined in the previous chapter, repeated activity can leave deep imprints. However, there is no simple extension to say that it can form the script for new actions. The emotional and physical marks from exhausting prison work were more likely to produce 'inhibition' rather than 'hibition'. They were more likely to leave an ex-prisoner bewildered and unprepared rather than somehow 'ready' for the society into which they were released. Repetitive hard labour or any repeated action over time, while always producing an effect in the person, leaves no guarantee of how that imprint will be revealed in the future. The work is performative in that it was an action in the present, but the policy-makers articulated the futuritive.

In 1932, an inquiry into prison work made the move between constative and futuritive even more explicit. Prison activities were now being more directly linked to the rehabilitation of the prisoner. Work was an integral part of daily life but also part of training for the future. It was 'real' but also unreal work; an 'as if' state preparing the prisoner for the 'reality' of life outside. This change was made more explicit in the 1948 Criminal Justice Act that ushered in a 'treatment and training' mission for the system. Number six in the prison rules now stated that 'the purposes of treatment and training of convicted prisoners shall be to establish in them the will to lead a good and useful life on discharge and to fit them to do so' (Simon, 1999, p. 6). The idea of creating a will inside a prisoner is similar to the earlier simplistic and essentialist notions of habit, but the desire to fit them for their 'good and useful' lives pushes this one stage further. The lack of 'fit' I believe is the situation leading to bewilderment. 'Fitting in' is the ambition to feel connected, part of and comfortable in a situation. The knowledge that you are 'intermeshed within your context' (to paraphrase Scheurich from chapter one) is what provides comfort and lack of bewilderment. 'Fitting someone' is also associated with making new suits or costumes for people. The fitting process is thus a kind of character creation. On the body of the old, a new attire/attitude will be hung.

It is important to emphasise that 'treatment and training' was a rhetorical flourish amounting to a statement of what the prison service wanted the system to be, not a description of what it was. However, at the heart of the rhetoric there was now developing the concept that prisons were a place of fitting – a place between the outside world and the new world. You enter from one side and are recreated within to be a new person who then leaves 'suited' for the world beyond. It is an in-between or liminal space (Turner, 1987). Of course, roles are rarely as complete and as easily crafted as this assumed they were. Although I believe the liminal nature of this experience makes prison an 'betwixt and between' (Schechner, 2002, p. 57) site of performance, the 'treatment and training' mission became a clear statement of a futuritive position. It explained the activities in terms of desired future actions. It was a position that somehow denied or forgot the performative.

As if purposefully to confound the comfort of a gradual progression from the constative to the futuritive, the 1970s saw a major shift in the discourse surrounding prison and punishment. There was a mood of pessimism in the field relating to the popular view that as far as the rehabilitation of offenders was concerned 'nothing worked' (Martinson, 1974). In response to this, the Prison Department moved away from the rhetoric of preparation to an emphasis on humane containment. The May Committee report of 1979 noted the general sense of disillusionment by stating that 'the rhetoric of treatment and training has had its day' (Simon, 1999, p. 8). Ironically, the report then went on to construct its own new and equally rhetorical objective for the service. The primary purpose of prison work now was to keep the prisoner occupied in a regime of 'positive custody'. This is perhaps the firmest statement of the constative position there has been. This is not to say that 'positive custody' does not function symbolically within a wider discourse, but rather, in this formulation, gone is the sense that the prison is a transitional space that rehearses the prisoner for re-entering society.

Although 'positive custody' was a major discursive turn for the prison service, the idea that the prison experience in general and work practices in particular should prepare prisoners for release certainly lingered. King and Morgan's argument, for example, implicitly accepts that prison has a function relating to rehearsal for the future. In a strong criticism of regimes in the seventies, they concluded that 'most prisoners are underemployed on tasks of little real value, in conditions that are a parody of the outside world' (King and Morgan, 1980, p. 15). This implies that conditions should do more than parody. They should be more authentic versions of the work environment on the outside. Unsurprisingly the use of the word 'parody' is significant for the argument I am making here. The representation of the 'real' that is needed to rehearse and train the prisoners is criticised as a poor copy. By being an unsatisfactory image, it only apes the outside. It is a pale imitation that by King and Morgan's logic can never instil the habit for the real. The danger implied is that a representation of the real outside world that does not accurately reflect it can act to mock that outside rather than encourage prisoners to adapt to it.

King and Morgan's argument underlines a certain naivety in the prison administration's desire to create an image or a version of work practice that reflects reality on the outside. Images, as I quoted above, are always partly 'phantasmic'. Whereas the mission to create a faithful copy is still the central aspiration of many of today's prison workers and commentators, it is perhaps an impossible one. Frances Simon in her book on prison work (Simon, 1999) poses the central question for the development of training in prisons as 'how far prison work should resemble outside work?' Her book advocates a vision of prison-based work and training where work does 'simulate' the outside environment as much as possible. She affirms the Prison Service Headquarters 1992 assertion that the first criterion for work in prison was that it was 'realistic compared with the work outside' (Simon, 1999, p. 184). The confusing relationship between this 'fiction' and the 'real' is a central concern of this chapter and one that I believe needs to be further problematised.

The 1990s

The history I have sketched above moved into the 1990s with a rejection of the pessimism of 'nothing works' and its replacement with a belief in new forms of 'offender rehabilitation' (see McGuire, 1995). This resulted in a reaffirmation of the futuritive function of prisons. In both the Woolf Report which followed the prison disturbances of 1990 (the Strangeways riot referred to in the introduction) and the subsequent Home Office White Paper *Custody, Care and Justice* (Home Office, 1991) a balance is sought between work that helps the prisoner have an 'active day' (Simon, 1999, p. 14) and that which will help on release. Both the constative of work as real in itself and the futuritive of work as a rehearsal for the 'real' outside are stated. It is in this context that Simon asserts her preference for regimes that prioritise preparation. All other types of work or approaches to training prisoners in her opinion must be incidental. Her analysis, however, also indicates the limitations and perhaps the impossibility of this vision. In interviews with prison staff, prisoners and ex-prisoners, the practicalities of this proposal are seriously undermined. The image of reality more often descends to parody than to the ideal to which she believes it should aspire.

The question is whether in an environment that is simultaneously 'real' and a representation, a person can ever be prepared or 'fitted' for an alternative outside 'real'? Does what is arguably the complex site of performance ever guarantee its relation to future actions? What does living in an artifice do for those returning to the 'original' that the artifice sought to imitate? These are of course crucial questions for applied-theatre practitioners as well as prison service managers. An interview done by Simon with a prison officer offers an approach to answering this query. In response to a question about the difference between the two worlds of work, this officer argued that:

> There's a great deal of difference [...] In prison it's artificial. Outside you're earning a salary, you're living a full life, in prison you're living part of a life. A lot of your life is very controlled, where it wouldn't be outside [...] This is a half-life. Things stop once you come into prison. (Simon, 1999, p. 121)

Both theatre workshops and prison workshops perhaps suffer from existing in this 'half-life'. However much work in a prison factory was constructed to relate to an outside-world location, therefore, it was always going to be experienced differently. The machines and the actual physical movements it takes to operate them do not create the meanings associated with the moment. Playing a role in a theatre performance or workshop similarly has no automatic relationship with that role in 'real life'. Work has no context-free properties, however much prison commentators over many years have hoped that it would. It is given meaning by the situation in which it happens, and the context of prison ensures that it is often one of control or lack of motivation. Living in the world of prison therefore creates its own set of experiences. It performs in the present tense, not as 'real' versions of the future. However much different parts of the prison regime – from education departments to work units – try to imitate real-world environments, the wider environment ensures that they are experienced as *prison* education departments and *prison* work units. This is not to dismiss the efforts of staff who change the ambience of their education departments or who put signs on walls calling a selection of prison buildings 'College X' and so forth. However, dressing up the prison is just as likely to encourage a prisoner to develop a cynical rejection of the parody as much as it is to offer a chance for her or him to engage in rehearsal for the outside world.

In this section, I have noted that work programmes in prison have been described historically as either a convenient way to expend time or as a rehearsal for work in the future. These two strands are presented as being in balance in official commentaries of the prison service today, but advocates of prison reform (for example Simon) urge a more fundamental shift, with work primarily existing as futuritive: as a preparation for release. Throughout this 'history' I have doubted the notion of work as rehearsal because the versions created assume that an image will in some way relate to that which has been copied. My doubt is a simple reiteration of the belief that there is an ambiguous relationship between sign and signified. In addition, it is a restatement of my assertion that actions are complex creations that cannot be packaged for neat exhibition at a later moment. Prison work I believe will therefore develop its own set of meanings without any guarantee that they will refer simply to related work contexts in the free world. Simon notes this in her follow-up of ex-prisoners when she states that:

> Employment at follow up was strongly linked to pre-sentence work record, and alternatively to pre-sentence occupational skills; but neither of these links were materially altered by what a person had done in prison. (Simon, 1999, p. 165)

The real/not real world of the prison, while it does have profound impact on those who pass through it, does not leave habits or create roles which can be simply played in the outside world. It is a transitional time in itself with its own set of meanings and experiences. It is performative. It creates its own liminal part-parody world which only sets people up to be dazzled and bewildered by the world they find once released. The web of relations and interconnections of previous work, although broken by the new prison experience, are in this example re-formed on return to the old.

So where does this leave the use of 'skills training' theatre in this context? In a space that I have framed as liminal, which attempts to create fictional worlds of work and education within it, the use of theatre would seem to further add to the artifice. Theatre workshops to train prisoners in skills for future employment become theoretically suspect. To claim once more that rehearsal in one context will somehow be repeated as activity in another seems to restate Simon's desire for prison to be a preparation for release only. To examine these questions I want to turn to two past projects dealing with issues of employment by the TIPP Centre and then finally to examine the theoretical assumptions made by a more recent initiative in which the centre has been involved.

The TIPP Centre

The Theatre in Prisons and Probation (TIPP) Centre was established in 1992 by myself and my colleague Paul Heritage. It operates from Manchester University Drama Department and it specialises in running theatre-based projects in the criminal-justice system. In recent years, it has also developed programmes for young people at risk of entering that system. TIPP prioritises participatory and workshop-based programmes with prisoners and young people and the organisation has built long-term relationships with a number of criminal-justice agencies. Some of its programmes have focused on specific offending-related issues (see Thompson, 1998, 1999), but it has also conducted a range of non-issue-specific creative projects.

The two projects

In March 1994 and September 1995 staff from the TIPP Centre ran two projects in Young Offender Institutions (YOIs) on issues of employment. Both consisted of a week of participatory drama workshops that ended with public performances attended by local employers, representatives of training agencies and various criminal-justice staff. The first took place in the recently opened Lancaster Farms YOI in partnership with East Lancashire Training and Enterprise Council (TEC) and Lancashire Probation Service, and the second was in the much older Hindley YOI in collaboration with Greater Manchester Probation Service (GMPS). YOIs hold young men between the age of sixteen and twenty-one, either convicted or awaiting trial. My commentary here is based on the two evaluation reports written by research staff of GMPS's Practice Development Unit (Shuttleworth, 1994; Poole, 1996) and also my role as facilitator of the first project and guest during the performance part of the second.

Before I go on to outline how I believe these projects engage with the debates I have already outlined, it is worth briefly explaining the exact nature of the theatre workshops that were run. Each day the groups of young men would take part in two approximately two-hour drama sessions. These included a range of exercises, starting with physical warm ups, moving through sculpting or still image work (Boal, 1992, pp. 164–91) and gradually arriving at role play and improvisation exercises. Whereas the general themes of the week were set (broadly the personal and social barriers to employment post-release) and the structure of the workshops organised, the men could develop the role plays and short scenes in directions they chose. Still sculpted images were created out of the bodies of participants on issues such as work, family and unemployment. These 'frozen' moments were then used to encourage the group to read what they saw and accept multiple readings of each moment. These varying readings would be validated and debated rather than fixed. Forum Theatre was used to encourage group members to intervene in the scenes they had created and suggest alternative actions (Boal, 1979). The aim was to help the young men to analyse and change the direction of the narratives they had constructed, but, in keeping with the framework that we used at the time, the forums were understood as giving the group opportunities to practice skills that might be useful in future employment situations. During the latter half of each week the open workshop structure became focused around the creation of a short performance for the end of the project. It became more theatre rehearsal than drama workshop. The ideal version of this process would be that the stories/aspirations of the men themselves were the subject matter of the presentations. Facilitators aimed to ease and dis-ease (dificilitate) this process, in order to push, challenge and engage the group, but ultimately the group were the directors/ scriptors.

Of course, as I hint above, this is both a report of, and an ideal version of the process. There are always glitches, changes and less-than-satisfactory moments. However, both in my experience of facilitating the first project and in reports from the facilitators of the second, both weeks progressed largely to plan and were received well by the groups of young men. Theatre exercises were central to both projects; however, only in the report on the second project (Poole,

1996) were these techniques seen as key. Along with our own assumptions about why the work was being done, it is here also that the work starts to be framed within some of the debates I have already touched upon. The report states that 'the project was [...] primarily addressing how alternative ways of working with particular challenging client groups could address issues of offending behaviour in a way that traditional methods had proved unsuccessful.' In addition it argues that 'drama is in essence a different way of delivering the same message' (Poole, 1996, p. 3). I agree with the assumption here that 'drama' is an appropriate way of working with challenging groups, however these statements also restrict the process to two particular discourses. 'Drama' is addressing behavioural issues and delivering messages. Clearly, my argument here is that these two constructions, although inherent in both projects, and behind much of the work of the TIPP Centre, do not adequately explain or contain the work.

Deliberate fiction

By placing theatre projects in a discourse of behaviour change, the report is on the one hand nodding to the strong demands on the Probation Service to use broadly cognitive behavioural forms of group work (Chapman and Hough, 1998); but also those projects unsurprisingly become understood within the 'prison as rehearser for release' frame. On the surface, this might be the obvious place for theatre projects, and the crossover between a service which was hoping to encourage groups to learn new behaviours, the prison that aims to prepare for life on release and the rehearsal model of the theatre workshop seems very strong. It seems evident that as part of a discourse that says prisons should provide a simulated environment for the practice of skills, theatre workshops should intervene to provide a literal moment of rehearsal. As I wrote in the introduction however, 'we need to question the deferred promise of rehearsal'. In

92

the evaluation reports on the process here, however, that promise is accepted as the rationale.

Traditionally prisons have responded to the demand to create simulated environments by copying the environmental fixtures. The machines, the floors, rooms, chalk boards, the carpets in the library, the altar in the chapel; they all dress the space. In constructing a training course, people have concentrated on the built environment rather than the human interactions. Theatre challenges and accepts the logic here. It accepts it by working in a fictional world, but it challenges it by saying proudly that this is simultaneously real and not real. It does not try desperately to create an image as close to reality as possible. In these applied-theatre prison projects, the environments created were deliberate fiction. Plastic chairs became office furniture and tables were bank counters. The parody is in the open because rather than hoping prisoners will learn skills from the artifice that can be transferred, theatre can and should use the artifice as a commentary on the 'real'. The theatre concentrates on the performative – that present-tense action – and therefore the play with and between realities is the point.

In prison work environments the men are always 'prisoners' doing work. However much the work is run like an outside business, with 'real' machines and 'real' orders, the context of prison life (the fact that you do not really get paid and the fact that you get fed whether you work or not) make this activity meaningful in its own terms and not as a preparation for something else. It creates its own set of connections for the person experiencing it. In prison theatre projects prisoners do not just engage with an 'unreal' situation, they are asked temporarily to transform themselves. They make a double shift from prisoner to actor and from actor to a specific role. The scenes created during the two projects discussed here involved prisoners as actors performing preparations for work at home, pressures domestically on finances, conflicts in the work environment and the difficulties in negotiating with your work colleagues. A multi-layered event that simultaneously related to real situations and was 'real' in the moment of execution. It was a complex and 'deliberate fiction' rather than a denied one. The participants continued to be prisoners while they played husband, son, boyfriend and colleague

93

engaging with problems, conversations and conflicts in these constructed worlds.

This theatrical process can therefore re-orientate the 'prison as rehearsal' proposition by creating a whole role play environment in which all problems, concerns and debates can be enacted. The way the projects have traditionally explained themselves however is that this process will generate skills and competencies that can be performed at similar social encounters in the future. However much these projects challenge the logic of the futuritive position, they still sit firmly within this framework. This is certainly how I as Director of the TIPP Centre would explain the work to partners and have written about it in the past (see Thompson, 1995). This book is deliberately trying to move beyond the narrowness of this analytical frame by doubting the assumptions made by the rehearsal model. By creating a total experience that allows people to enact and discuss the outside world, do they automatically develop skills that they can use when they are released? Can we really hope that a role played in the prison theatre workshop will create immunity from the bewilderment that can arise in the transition to a new place?

There are many examples of interventions with young people, prisoners and others designated as having 'behavioural problems' that use the training in social skills model, assuming that these new abilities will become transferable to the outside (Goldstein, 1994; Hollin, 1990; Rose, 1998). A broadly cognitive behavioural model insists that the identification of a skill deficit can be followed up by practice of a pro-social replacement which will then be readily available for reproduction outside the group-work room. Reframing this within a more explicitly theatrical model, a problem with a particular real-life scenario can be overcome by rehearsing an alternative script of that moment so that it can then be (re)performed later. As I argue in chapter one, there is an assumption that humans store complete skills or roles as a resource that can then be called up cognitively at the right future moment. As an approach to analysing this example of applied-theatre work, I believe it restricts our understanding and in fact does not do justice to the impact of the workshops.

Whereas scholars in this field claim considerable research support (Gendreau, 1996), it is also noted that many projects suffer from 'the failure of generalisation of gain' (Goldstein and Glick, 1994, p. 100). Put simply, the impressive results within the group-work room often are not translated to 'gains' on the outside. In the context of this chapter, prisoners who learn new skills, competencies, roles or behaviours in the world of the prison do not automatically translate these to the free world. I believe that drama-based work offers the closest possibility for the futuritive model to be credible. The extended deliberate fiction engages people in a much fuller version of the practice of human interactions. However, if the workshop is understood within the terms of the previous chapter – as an example of the intentional playing with action fragments – its nuances become more apparent.

The group of men who entered the workshop on the first day of the first of the two projects looked scared. Their bodies were tense, taut and the words they uttered always seemed to struggle out of their mouths. The expectations of the prison space had not prepared them for this experience. The first exercises added to their sense of bewilderment. They were clearly fitted into the prison in different degrees. Several were swaggeringly comfortable; others seemed more nervously vulnerable. All however were wired into the performance conventions of prison. They sloped, smoked and spoke in similar repeated movement patterns. They now had to negotiate a new environment. This process required them to detach themselves from some intergroup structures of meaning and hold on to others. It offered fresh sets of unexpected actions for them to engage with. It required them to set up an unfamiliar mediation system. Occasionally you could witness this happening almost physically as a group member would search his peers' faces in disbelief to see if they were actually going to do what was asked of them. Existing conventions seemed to snap as the men got to their feet to participate in a game. 'I can't believe I'm doing this' expressed the dislocation between the expectations of one context and the 'habits' of another. Their stilted physical participation at first betrayed the marks of previous actions and bodily expectations. The theatre workshop however started to create its own meaning structure in the moment. Over the full week, this led to moments of physical exhaustion, riotous laughter, uninhibited play and forceful debate. The single word used by the group most to describe this was the word most often applied to drug-induced highs. The week was a 'buzz'. Initial bewilderment was reformed to become a new meaning-creating environment – an environment that insisted on and valued participation, fun, debate, physical action and creativity.

If you watch a slow-motion film of ice forming, complex crystals gradually evolve in a criss-cross pattern of connections. A shard will move from one point to another and this then repeats itself in an increasingly elaborate design. It becomes fixed and recognisable as the connection is made, not before. Although never as uniform and predictable as this, the transition from the crystallised interactions of the prison world to the new formations offered by the theatre project experience undergoes a similar process. These are the 'webs of significance' of cultural anthropologists such as Clifford Geertz (1973, p. 5), but I am using a glacial metaphor because I am specifically interested in how they break down and reform. During this first project connections appeared slowly at first, and became more complex and elaborate as the week evolved. As with the movement from outside into prison or prison to the outside, these crystallised structures melt and reform at different rates. The melting is the time of bewilderment, but also the melting and reforming is a process that repeatedly happens during a 'heat'-inducing theatre workshop. Whole roles, habits or behaviours do not become reproduced from the person outwards. The shape of the crystal does not exist before it is formed. Activity and the meaning given to that activity are constructed between people (see Salomon, 1993). A set of connections only half melts in the moment of transition and this makes the reforming of the more familiar links easier. The men in Simon's book (Simon, 1999) found employment post-release that was very similar to the work they had had before prison. They had reconnected themselves into that system because the structures that were created in their prison experience did not find links to moments outside.

The theatre workshop therefore needs to be understood not as simple rehearsal but as an intense experience that creates a network of

96

meaningful activities in the present. To repeat a phrase that Norman Uphoff used to describe development projects that had surprising and hard-to-measure dynamism and persistence, it creates a form of 'social energy' (Uphoff, 1996, pp. 357–87). That energy can melt certain relations and kindle others. It can be linked to the notion of 'spontaneous communitas' used by Turner to describe deep forms of personal interaction (Turner, 1982, p. 47). It is a force that can potentially leave positive marks over the physical and emotional experiences with which a person enters the workshop. The notion of social energy blurs the lines between the performative and the futuritive, opening the possibility that members of the group could 'fit' themselves into similar networks in the future. They are unlikely to become actors, or the fathers, mothers, sons and brothers that they played. The experience of play, story telling, physical activity, a certain person or a particular phrase however might find meaning in a later situation and leave less likelihood of the dislocation of bewilderment. The sets of alliances, conventions and systems of meaning-making that are developed within the prison can profoundly affect a person, and although certain will disappear on release many are desperately reproduced. Again, I am not saying the behaviour is re-performed, rather the connection is remade. The theatre workshop offers a radically new set of intense connections, some of which might linger or reform in a new situation on the outside. They are not whole roles or discreet skills but patterns of interactions and meaning, and therefore reproduction will only ever be a partial reforming. One ice crystal while having similar shapes and angles will never be the same as another.

I once met a young woman ex-prisoner in the street with whom I had worked on a theatre project in prison. She proudly told me how thanks to the project, she had decided to take a nursery nurse course and she was now in the process of completing it. This is not transference of skill. The drama had not rehearsed the behaviour of 'nursery nurse' that she was now performing on the outside. Instead, some positive part of the structure of meaning creation in that workshop found resonance in that new 'real world' opportunity. A phrase, a movement, a smile or a dialogue could have lingered and found a point to reconnect with the outside. The workshop had perhaps built some of the strands that had given her a bridge across bewilderment.

Self-esteem and confidence

One of the indicators used by both reports to analyse the success of these projects was change in self-esteem. Specifically the second project used Rosenberg's (1965) 'Self-Esteem Scale' in the form of a questionnaire filled before and after the course by the project participants. The logic was that any evidence of a rise in self-esteem should indicate success, as low self-esteem was viewed as a precursor to lack of employment and further offending. Both projects, according to an analysis of these questionnaires, demonstrated a rise in the self-esteem of all participants. Interviews with staff also seemed to back this up, with many noting greater confidence in the young people on completion of the project. Poole quotes the governor of Hindley as saying that 'it was hard to believe that these were the same youngsters who, just a few weeks before the project had hard-held aggressive opinions about education, prison and life generally' (Poole 1996, p. 27).

Again this is not to be dismissed, and my experience of the two projects would back up this immense change in general openness and confidence amongst the men. However, I think it would be wrong to simply conflate a rise in self-esteem with the argument I am making for the impact of creating new structures of meaning. In addition, it would be wrong to see increase in self-esteem as evidence of the value of the futuritive model. The very variability of self-esteem (measured so easily by Rosenberg's scale) makes me suspicious that it can be defined as a property emanating from a person. It really should be understood as a property of the interrelation of the person with the situation they are in. The connections a person might make to an activity that in itself affirms them as significant, worthy, humorous or valuable creates a sense of self-esteem in that moment. Take the

98

person back to a completely different environment and that connection can easily be broken and a new 'esteem' be formed. Of course, levels of esteem changed from the prison environment to the theatre workshop. The question however should be how that sense might linger and not be extinguished. A rise in self-esteem was not a property that once possessed could be taken with the prisoners wherever they went. It is only sustainable if it is fitted into a structure that welcomes it. Whereas this reconnecting of lingering experiences is difficult, it is not always a naive aspiration. The woman who became the nursery nurse was perhaps an example of this.

So, although the reporting on these projects conceptualised them in a similar way to the historical demand for a futuritive function for prison work, this framework must be challenged as limiting. By claiming to deliver packaged chunks of human attributes ready for future display (for example, assertiveness or self-esteem) theatre workshops are aligning themselves to an over-simplistic model (see Thompson, 1999a; Rose, 1998). Human activity is not constructed from 'off the peg' resources which we carry in neat compartments or can pass on in a calculable deterministic fashion (see Landy, 1993). Our repertoires are constructed and performed in a more complex, shifting and adaptive way. Taking on a character in a role play creates a network of meanings and resonance in the process of playing. It creates a web of multiple connections at physical, discursive and emotional levels. This process can leave web remnants, threads that seek new connections or make an imprint on a person. However, it will not leave a complete role competency for future regurgitation.

Although I am criticising the vastly oversimplified and I believe optimistic concept of rehearsal-based behaviour change, both of the TIPP projects in the Young Offender Institutions did indicate an implicit recognition of some of these problems by making a radical departure from other employment-related prison projects. This was precisely in the area of transference from one context to another and of how to sustain impact. The idea of transition to the outside was given a new slant by encouraging the outside – in the form of employers' groups and training providers – to come in. This happened in both projects in the creation of a final performance.

Performance – delivering a message?

Poole's second analysis of the use of theatre was that it was a 'different way of delivering the same message' (Poole, 1996, p. 3). This again is a narrow definition of theatre processes and consigns performance to a one-way movement of information. Although theatre can be a monologic experience – from actors to spectators – it is false to regard 'messages' as a fixed construct easily transferred from one group to another. As a reading of the end performances, it severely limits and misreads a much more complex process.

Each project ended with a presentation of a short improvised play to an invited audience. From the outset, it was agreed by all agencies working on the projects that employment should not be seen as a problem for the prisoners alone. It was not only their lack of skills, experience or motivation that diminished their chances of finding work but also the barriers constructed by society in its prejudices against ex-prisoners. The performance thus became an important moment through which the impression that employers had of prisoners could be challenged. As many employers were invited as possible so that the young men could make a direct link with them. The logic was that this might prove useful in future job hunting and that the positive impression of these 'prisoners' could affect individual employers' prejudices. The report on the first project (Shuttleworth, 1994, p. 13) states how there was 'an enthusiastic and open exchange of views between the audience and offenders'. The report on the second expands on this by noting that:

> The role the offenders adopted as performers gave them authority to speak to the audience and particularly the employers, in a way that probably neither side had experienced prior to this. (Poole, 1996, p. 14)

She goes on to describe this as an 'unusual dialogue' (Poole, 1996, p. 14). It was unusual because certain conventions of dialogue were undermined. Prisoners spoke to and asked questions of free people. An audience was permitted to speak to performers, and potential employees were questioning future employers. Each of these interactions was unfamiliar and perhaps unnerving for some. The plays and the subsequent discussions thus created their own new structures of meaning. It was bewildering because it set up systems of talk and rules of engagement that were unfamiliar in situations of employment and in the prison. 'Offenders' were not offenders, they were performers and therefore in that role a different discursive act could be performed. One Education Guidance Officer from the community who came to the event in Hindley is quoted as saying that she now 'realised what prejudices offenders are up against' and that it would help her 'in the future when dealing with clients' (Poole, 1996, p. 27). Although she frames this within the familiar futuritive model, it is not a script, skill or behaviour that has been learnt. The structure of the engagement has crystallised certain connections that she believed could be reformed later. Applied theatre in this context was operating within a performative model, which in itself challenged the constative and futuritive emphases of other programmes. Here it was not ignoring the desire for change in the future, but celebrating an action in the present.

The question that must be asked following on from the above is how the performative is linked to the futuritive? Is the 'promise of performance' (Heritage, 1998) ever kept? How can connections be carried between different situations, and what allows them to be reformed? If a connection created in one particular moment contains meanings which out of the moment melt away, and if in a different moment new forms of interaction with their own structures are created, how can the positive impact of one experience be carried forward to impact on the formation of the conventions governing a new one? I think the performance helps answer this. First, work in prisons in the UK is framed predominantly in a discourse of change of the prisoner and not change of the outside world. This as I have discussed in comparison to the criminal-justice system in Brazil is a particular construction of prison policy in this context. This project made a bold attempt to reverse this by inviting into the prison those outside so that their understandings and practices could be challenged. Positive 'fitting in' by ex-prisoners can only be at all possible if the structure of the society to which they return can contain them, accept them and build new networks for them. The presence of the employers at the performances at least demonstrated willingness for some people to start forcing the bridges between the prison and the outside. They were not hoped for but were built in a small way in the moment of each performance. In participating in this activity, in realising the connections, the promise is given shape and substance.

Second, the projects, and above all the performances, were often described by prisoners as a 'buzz'. Prison usually creates a very rigid pattern of conventions that have a withering effect on the senses. The networks that create meanings in our lives can be rich, fluid and complex, but in the artificial world of prison, they can be very strict and restricting. The bewilderment on leaving prison, as noted at the beginning of this chapter, is often derived from the dazzling impact of an 'overdose of sensory perception'. If an experience such as a drama workshop or a performance can produce the feeling of 'buzz' – communitas or social energy – in a group, they might be more tuned in or awakened to a diverse sensory experience and therefore less likely to be affected by the overdose of bewilderment. The drama experience could become the adjusting or sensitising transitory moment between the prison and the rupture to the outside. The performance in particular can demonstrate the potential for those connections to be made by bringing together 'real' people in this complex and constructed environment.

Partnership 97

The importance of bringing the outside in was the central tenet of a project that started in HMP Buckley Hall in 1997. It was timed neatly with the arrival of the new Labour government and attempted to claim a space for prison programmes to fit with the wider concerns for employment training with excluded communities that marked the rhetoric and policy of that administration. Buckley Hall was an adult male medium-security prison near Rochdale to the north of Manchester with prisoners from across the north-west of England.

This project was based on a post-Woolf-report (Woolf and Tumin, 1991) ethos that 'prisons cannot do their work without the active support of the communities which they serve' (Lateral Associates, 1999, p. 19). It aimed to bring a range of community organisations into the prison to work with the prisoners, treating them as part of the region's long-term unemployed. On release, the vision was that the ex-prisoners would continue to be clients of and supported by those agencies. The emphasis on classifying the inmates as 'long-term unemployed' ties this project to the particular policy dynamic of the time, and sought to lever a new source of funding for prison work programmes. Where this project made a break with the rhetorical constructions of the past was that it seemed to doubt that the prison could create the space that would provide the rehearsal ground for a prisoner's future. In a project proposal document that simultaneously described and advocated for the project, the 'world of the prison' was outlined as having 'little interest or relevance to life outside' (Lateral Associates, 1999, p. 6). Like Simon (1999) it recognised that 'incarceration would almost certainly maintain, if not amplify' the special needs of prisoners (Lateral Associates, 1999, p. 4). However, it did not seek to construct new and 'more accurate' employment training zones within the prison. It did not aspire to prison work becoming a representation of the outside, because it explicitly saw that this was difficult if not impossible to achieve. Instead, it urged the transition to be made by the community integrating its services into the prison itself. It urged 'community driven regimes' (Lateral Associates, 1999, p. 7) that blur the distinctions between the two worlds.

The TIPP Centre ran weekly theatre workshops as part of this project from the moment it started. Like the earlier projects discussed here, these used theatre to discuss and debate issues of employment. Whereas it would be wrong to claim that these transformed the limited discourse of rehearsal and behaviour change, they were perhaps more dynamically situated as moments to discuss the problems of transition rather than prepare people for it. Although the Lateral Associates document did claim that this was partly a simulation exercise, where participants were 'able to experience as closely as possible some of the challenges of leaving prison' (Lateral Associates, 1999, p. 11), it

103

also framed the work as a point at which 'the complexities of life after release were frankly discussed' (Lateral Associates, 1999, p. 29).

By blurring the lines that mark the prison as a separate arena from the outside world, the project was a radical departure from previous formulations. It took the shock of departure, the dislocation of moving from one tight structure of inter-group relations to another, as the central problem for prison work and employment programmes. The high rate of reoffending (65% to 85% according to the Lateral document, p. 1) was positioned as a failure of the prison experience to offer any new points of connection. Prisoners either rediscovered old systems, networks and alliances, or they maintained the structures and codes etched out in the 'half-life' of prison. This project sought to gradually work people into a new environment at a point before they were launched into the outside world.

As I mentioned above, the project document I have been referring to was both a report and an exercise in advocacy. It simultaneously described what had been happening and what would or should be happening. In addition the project as it existed in 1997 was both 'real' and also a pilot (a rehearsal) for an anticipated larger and more system-wide approach to employment training for soon-to-be released prisoners. It therefore existed in much the same discursive divisions that I have been describing throughout this chapter. For this reason, as an exercise in advocacy, it is important to examine it in the wider context in which it was situated. Because 'prison' exists at a symbolic level in the popular imagination as a place apart, a separate zone or as somewhere deliberately designed to disconnect people from society, it is very hard to construct a competing rhetoric of the prison as part of and connected to that community. It is even harder to maintain that individuals, groups and employers have a responsibility to enter and engage with the space. Prison is more often articulated as banishment from, not a means to reconnect to society. Although the vision of 'community driven regimes' was thus a powerful move, it actually required a much greater challenge to the historically and culturally dominant understanding of prison as the excision of the unwanted from the public realm. This project was making a bold statement; but as has been emphasised in this chapter, the success of a pilot or a rehearsal does not mean that similar activity will be repeated elsewhere. The TIPP Centre, in aligning itself to this moment of advocacy, was situating an applied-theatre practice within a particular and contested understanding of prison work programmes. This was sustained for a few years and certainly provided a fruitful area of practice for the organisation. However, as with all applied-theatre programmes, this placed TIPP within a policy structure that shifted as the orthodoxy changed. The move to 'education' being seen as the sole priority for regimes in the early part of the new millennium provides a new challenge for theatre practitioners, while also threatening the viability of the employment-based projects.

Conclusion

The historical divisions between the proponents of prison work experience as a place to prepare people for a more positive life on release and those that saw it as an appropriate way to pass time at best and be punished at worst, have placed a discursive boundary around the field which limited the way that projects in prison could be described. They were either a good way for prisoners to spend their sentence or a rehearsal for skills to be used in the future. Theatre projects have clearly positioned themselves within these alternating and competing approaches to understanding prison work. However, by focusing on the point of transition − a moment often experienced as bewilderment − I have tried to show that prison does not fall so neatly between the two models. The prison fictional worlds of workshops and education colleges cannot be faithful copies of the real. They can only set up their own systems of meanings that are likely to bear a confused and partial resemblance to similar activities on the outside. They are as likely to parody as provide a positive place to rehearse for 'real world' experience. However, prison cannot only be seen as a place of containment − 'positive' or otherwise − which will leave no impact on the future of the prisoner. The places and the projects in them are performative. The structures of meaning, conventions, codes and particular interactions will leave lingering marks on the prisoner. Some they will struggle to shake off in an attempt to reform old structures within their families and communities, others they will desperately seek to maintain to provide a sense of security.

Into this picture of shifting structures and situated impact come the projects I have described here. This chapter has attempted to demonstrate that they cannot be understood simply as part of the rhetoric of behaviour rehearsal. Instead, they must be framed as 'real' moments that construct systems of interaction and meaning that can compete and create a friction with the surrounding prison environment. That friction is linked to Uphoff's 'social energy' and in the intense experience of events such as theatre projects, it could be claimed that this force melts the rigidity of certain social interactions. Certainly, it is in this less tangible area of analysis that the complexity of the theatre workshop or performance event needs to be positioned, rather than the neat and over-simplistic terrain of rehearsals for the future. When theatre practitioners rely on the discursive formulations of the futuritive model, they not only simplify the process behind the work but also deny much of its power.

Finally, the presence of employers and other agencies during the performances blurred and confused the distinction between the prison as rehearsal space and prison as a separate but 'real' space. By working to bring these groups into the prison in the Partnership 1997 project, an opportunity to link the inside world to the outside was being developed. Although this bridging will never be a neat reconnection of whole attitudes, roles or skills, this project could have developed points of positive continuity for prisoners. Like all others however, it needed to be examined when it was operational, and the practice needed to be explored in relation to the restrictions provided by the wider discursive boundaries of the criminal justice system. In 2002 there are many employment programmes with vulnerable communities that use theatre, but the Partnership project as such no longer exists. It offered an innovative direction that could have generated more carefully planned transitions during which the dangerous meltdown of bewilderment might have been averted. However, as a product of a particular political and social moment, it was lost as priorities were altered and understanding of the 'best approach' to offender rehabilitation changed.

A final point on two discourses

The constative tradition of prison as an act in itself and the futuritive tradition of prison as a rehearsal for future good citizenship have now become the poles around which the competing rhetoric of 'tough retribution' and cognitive behavioural group work based rehabilitation have coalesced (see Chapman and Hough, 1998). This chapter, rather than seeking a position between this unhelpful dichotomy, has tried to articulate the performative aspect of particular interventions. However, this dichotomy is very hard to escape and therefore undoubtedly people seeking to devise theatre projects in prisons in the UK will be forced to frame their work within these discursive boundaries: the project as a 'good way to spend time' or one that 'offers useful skills for release'. It would be unhelpful to say that we must not engage with these debates, as an abstentionist approach can mean that no practice takes place. Applied theatre went through those gates, even when anxious about the compromises that might arise. It is a form of theatre that negotiates with the specific moments of social practice without denying that this is potentially problematic and challenging. Initially the theatre projects discussed above were described in futuritive terms, but I believe their impact was far more complex. However, in the UK in 2002 the deferred promise of behaviour rehearsal is still admired and therefore prison theatre practitioners may need to continue to use it as their opening pledge with the prison authorities. We must accept however that 'like all promises they won't be kept' (Phelan, 1993, p. 24) and the struggle to create a range of other possibilities must continue to be discovered from analysis of the actual work. In a small way, this chapter has attempted to do just that. It has sought to offer a way of seeing theatre in prison rehabilitation programmes that avoids the tendency of

107

accounts to simplify the richness offered by the experience. My account is of course as partial as any other and is an attempt at creating a shape that could easily melt when confronted with a different example.

The next chapter continues this theme. It discusses the tension between lines, versions and approaches to applied theatre where the operation of 'hidden' orthodoxies is questioned in the rich context of one of the poorest countries in the world.

Chapter Three
Atelier Théâtre Burkinabé: applied theatre and the bourgeois gentilhomme

This chapter moves away from practice in the UK to explore a radically different environment in which theatre has been applied. The work I outline in this chapter would more traditionally be referred to as 'theatre for development', and it is this terminology that is used by the company who will be the focus for the argument here. I include its practice as one that can also be called 'applied theatre' for several reasons. First, labelling a practice with one name does not seek to dismiss the relevance or appropriateness of the other. For example, at the International Drama Education Conference in Bergen in July 2001 Albert Wandago, a Kenyan delegate, noted that he now preferred the term 'applied theatre' for a practice that was previously categorised as 'theatre for development'. It was to him a more open and less prescriptive term. The phrase 'applied theatre' is thus gaining currency and is being used interchangeably in a range of settings. Second, as noted in the preface 'community-based theatre' practices in places such as the UK have for too long been split from the practice of 'theatre for development' in 'third world' settings as though these distinct sites had created two different forms of theatre practice that had very little in common. Somehow the 'civilised' West/North avoids or denies the need for development. 'Applied theatre' is thus used as an inclusive term that aims to develop dialogues between practices that have much to learn from each other. I do not deny the differences, but I believe that varieties of participatory theatre work do have discursive and practical similarities that are worth exploring.

This chapter therefore takes the dialogue I speak of above as the starting point for questions about the adaptations in theatre practice that appear or are made necessary by a particular setting. This is done specifically around theatre projects that are in some way inspired by the work of Augusto Boal. His work has of course been identified as a major influence on much of the practice referred to in this book. However, this chapter starts to ask how specific settings can reveal where that influence exists as orthodoxy and where it is offered as a flexible point of departure. If applying theatre requires a respect for the setting into which we take the practice, we have to question the type of theatre we bring. Does an insistence on Boalian practice include unchanging principles, or is it a totally transformable array of techniques? We also of course need to work backwards and be aware of how certain settings have influenced the style of theatre that both take place in them and is taken to them. Prisons force the theatre work to adapt or change. Conflict situations require different approaches. When therefore should the practice happily transform itself, and when should it hold on to a fixed or 'correct' approach? What are the limits to contingency in applied theatre? In this chapter, Francophone West Africa becomes the challenging site for theatre application. The country of Burkina Faso is shown to raise questions about the principles of what is, at first appearance, the familiar practice of 'Forum Theatre' (Boal, 1979). This chapter thus asks which principles of applied-theatre practice are malleable and should adapt to their context, and which can be taken as givens regardless of setting. If, as I stated in the introduction, applied theatre seeks breaks from the past, can it claim adherence to any specific methodology?

'Lift the veil [...] so that the fête can start'

Like the bourgeois gentleman of Molière who made prose without knowing it, ATB also came to practice forum theatre before discovering that a Brazilian by the name of Augusto Boal had elaborated a theory of Theatre of the Oppressed based on the forum theatre technique. (ATB, 1998b. Trans. author)

Today, the moment to lift the veil and discover our parental ties has at last come; this will raise the moon so that the fête can start: the fête of the reunion of modern theatre with traditional Voltaic performance. Our ambition will be to throw out footbridges in order to recreate a lost unity, clean the room of prejudices and misunderstandings, and to resolutely take our place in the circle of the dance. (Prosper Kompaoré quoted in Duhamel and Bordet, 1994, p. 14. Trans. author)

In order to answer the questions I outline above, this chapter will borrow from a particularly vibrant and contentious area of theatre research and practice. It will make a link between interculturalism and applied theatre in order to develop the debate. I will argue that the discussions surrounding intercultural performance can inform analysis of the relationship between applied theatre and the practices encountered in non-theatre spaces or places. If applied theatre is a moment of interaction between two fields where different norms and understandings of practice meet, then research into the complex exchange between different cultural forms displayed in intercultural work can support analysis of these moments. I propose to take a particular concept from interculturalism and use it as a method to prise open dilemmas in applied theatre. Although this does not seek to minimise the differences between the two fields, I do believe applied theatre practice has a great deal to learn from the writing in this area. Much of the argument I make in this book is that the disciplines into which theatre seeks to apply itself are cultural practices that have their own explanatory discourses. They are not neutral containers into which theatre is placed. The problems of synthesis, cultural exchange and power, debated so vigorously by writers such as Rustom, Bharucha (1990, 2000) and Patrice Pavis (1992, 1996), offer useful frameworks for the critical engagement that is sought here.

To explore this further I am going to analyse the practice of a theatre company that I believe is both intercultural and applied. The tension of the intercultural will therefore be existing alongside some of the concerns of theatre application. The chapter will examine the practice and the claims made by the group Atelier Théâtre Burkinabé (ATB). ATB is a large theatre organisation based in Ouagadougou, the capital of Burkina Faso in West Africa. It is chosen because it both confuses some of the simple oppositions established in debates over interculturalism and because it has challenged many of the assumptions which I believe are common to applied theatre. It is also my focus because I have a professional connection with the company going back to 1996. I have visited its International Festival for Theatre for Development twice and managed a large-scale training project with the company funded from the UK. As with any debate about both interculturalism and applied theatre, my position in relation to this practice is a vital part of the problems and tensions that I seek to discuss.

The concept I will use to frame my discussion offers a valuable means of analysing and commenting on the applied-theatre field. It is taken from Philip Zarrilli's discussion of a Kathakali production of *King Lear* (Zarrilli, 1992) where he quotes the ethnographer James Clifford's method of interpreting the breakdown of metanarratives with either a 'narrative of entropy or loss [... as] an inescapable, sad truth' or 'a more ambiguous "Caribbean" experience [...] reconceived as inventive process or creolised "interculture"' (Zarrilli, 1992, p. 16; Clifford, 1988, pp. 14–15). I want to take the former and use it to refer to an analytic strategy that understands the meeting of two cultural practices as inevitably involving the diminishing or weakening of one form of practice. According to this view, the interaction creates a loss of a tradition. This is relevant to applied theatre as it offers a commentary on the problem of what type of theatre form to use in projects and the fear of how the theatre practice will be influenced by the new environment or community. The meeting is often spoken of as a compromise of the art form when faced with a social institution, agency or a particular population's demands. The 'Caribbean experience' is also a useful narrative because it implies that applying theatre can be an approach that enriches practices through the creation of new synthesised forms. The interaction leads to inventiveness and new creative possibilities, not the dilution of 'artistic integrity'. Whereas Zarrilli states he has chosen the more ambiguous 'Caribbean experience' (Zarrilli, 1992, p. 17) to frame his argument about an example of intercultural practice, I aim to concentrate on the 'narrative of loss' to question different moments of an engagement with ATB during the UK-funded project. This is not because I believe that this is the most appropriate framework in which to conceive its work, but because it is an interpretative narrative that is used explicitly and implicitly in many discussions of applied theatre. By highlighting how this discourse is ultimately limiting and distorting, a greater understanding of the richness of ATB's practice and the wider possibilities for theatre's engagement with new and diverse social arenas can be realised.

This chapter will start with an outline of the history and background of ATB. It will then examine how ATB has explained its work and particularly its relationship with the practice of Augusto Boal. I will question why it has sought to distance its practice from that of Boal, while at the same time adopting many of Boal's forms. Next, it will examine how the Boalian form of Forum Theatre has been changed (lost?) by the practice of ATB and the context of Burkina Faso. Finally, the chapter argues that these changes and the actual practice of ATB are far more complex than a 'narrative of loss' permits. The discursive construction of its work will be examined in relation to the variety of competing and partially determining audiences. This is particularly in reference to its position as a major organisation in the development community in Burkina Faso and its links with international donors. My role as festival audience member and an indirect representative of an international agency will therefore be included in this analysis.

ATB – history and context

Burkina Faso (formerly Upper Volta) is a landlocked country in the centre of West Africa, approximately one thousand kilometres from the coast. Whereas the southern regions bordering Ghana, the Côte D'Ivoire, Togo and Benin are lush and fertile, the northern regions are part of the dry Sahelian belt. Here the land is continually being encroached by the Sahel desert, making subsistence farming extremely precarious. Although there are many reasons for the economic plight of the nation, its geographical position has been a major factor in making Burkina Faso one of the poorest countries in the world (Duhamel and Bordet, 1994).

Across the 45 districts of Burkina there are some 60 different ethnic groups contributing to a population of nearly nine million people (Morrison, 1991). There are 17 major languages and 3 are designated as national languages (Mooré, Dioula and Fulfulde) with French providing the language of administration. Many of the educated members of ATB are French-speakers, although the plays it performs are often in Mooré, the language that predominates in the capital Ouagadougou. Burkina Faso was as Upper Volta part of French colonial rule in West Africa. It became a colony in 1896 and was integrated into French West Africa in 1904. It almost disappeared in 1932 when its different parts were divided between other regional colonies (Spaas, 2000, p. 232). It was reunified under the French Union in 1947 and was finally renamed Upper Volta in 1959 before formally gaining its independence in 1960. Successive post-independence military regimes culminated in a coup by the charismatic Captain Thomas Sankara in 1983. His rule was characterised by a radical agenda including wide-scale education initiatives, a huge programme of tree planting and an anti-imperialist stance in the international arena. Part of his legacy was the changing of the country's name from the colonial Upper Volta to Burkina Faso, meaning the 'land of dignified (or upright) men'. His campaigns against corruption and attempts to reduce the salaries of public-sector workers alienated certain sections of the population and when, in 1987, his regime started faltering, Sankara was killed during a coup led by his right-hand man, Blaise Compaoré. Compaoré remains the president at time of writing in 2002.

Burkina Faso is a largely rural country whose more than seven thousand villages rely on subsistence farming. There is a high level of illiteracy, particularly amongst women, and a relatively high infant mortality rate (183 per 1,000 births in 1990 – Morrison 1991, p. 88). In this context ATB has created theatre that aims to put itself 'at the service of development' (sign outside ATB headquarters quoted in Morrison, 1991, p. 110) since 1978. The implications of this phrase are explored later in this chapter. Today it has a large base in the Gougin region of the capital Ouagadougou with its own 300 seat open-air theatre, an indoor theatre, accommodation for trainees and an administrative base. While it is involved in a wide range of activities, it is best known for touring Forum Theatre productions on a range of development issues across the country, for training new theatre groups and for hosting the International Festival for Theatre for Development every two years. It was during this festival in 1996 that I first encountered its work (see Thompson, 1999b for a review of the festival).

ATB was established on 18 June 1978 and now has a repertoire of over fifty shows on social and development themes. On average, it performs ten times per year in the large cities and about thirty times in smaller towns and villages. It has also attended many international theatre festivals. ATB's history is explained by its director Prosper Kompaoré as fitting into three distinct phases. Although the work of the current phase is of central concern to this chapter, it is important to outline the first two to illustrate the development and change in ATB's work. The first phase is called the Rural Theatre, and this period lasted between 1979 and 1981. This was partly stimulated by the large-scale project funded by the Ford Foundation in 1979 that sought to assist a government relocation scheme in the Volta Valley. These low valleys had been opened up for habitation after a programme to eradicate the tsetse fly had been successful. However, the local rural people had been reluctant to return for fear of infection. The government approached the Amateur Voltaic Theatre (as ATB was called at the time) to help explain the scheme, which the company did by writing a short play and performing it to numerous villages across the area. The Rural Theatre phase gave way to a period called District or Area Theatre (Théâtre de Quartier) that occupied the company between 1981 and 1983. During this phase the company performed mostly in and around the city of Ouagadougou, creating theatrical interventions in the important urban issues of the day. These shows included participatory warm-up sessions and a form of dialogue with the audience that encouraged their direct intervention in the theatrical action.

During this period, ATB became more familiar with the work of Augusto Boal and started to adopt some of his techniques in its performance work. This relationship became more explicit in the current phase of its work where it now uses the expression 'Forum Theatre' to describe its approach. This is clearly of central importance to this chapter both because of the significance of Boal to the practice of applied theatre and the fact that this is an intercultural meeting of an African company with a practice that originated in Brazil. This Forum Theatre phase of ATB's work is still developing and growing today. From its base in Ouagadougou, ATB now tours authored works and company-created shows on development themes, takes commissions from governmental and non-governmental organisations for new programmes and trains theatre groups from across the country in Forum Theatre. Since 1984, it has created interactive 'Forum' shows on a huge range of issues including vaccination, early pregnancy, diarrhoea, latrines, water cleanliness, HIV/AIDS, dental hygiene and family planning. The strong relationship between ATB, donor agencies and government departments evidenced in its early work in the Rural Theatre phase is continued today in the major role that ATB has within a range of local and national development initiatives. One of the central points of interest here is that ATB's theatre, rather than being a marginal activity within the different social arenas in which it operates, is a significant and vital part of the execution of donor and governmental programmes. From its centre in Ouagadougou, ATB has a very particular partnership with a range of agencies that provides a complex and challenging model for discussions of applied theatre.

ATB – the bourgeois gentilhomme

The first part of my questioning of ATB is focused on the relationship of its theatre to the Theatre of the Oppressed tradition of Augusto Boal (1972). Here we have an extraordinary intercultural moment. A Burkinabé theatre company borrows from the work of a Brazilian director. What this borrowing constitutes and how it is discussed by ATB is central to the argument presented here. There is an obvious complication in that the interaction of forms takes place between practices from two very different postcolonial settings. Writing on postcolonialism tends to focus on the complex interrelation of the colonising centre with the ex-colonial periphery (see, for example, Lazarus, 1999). Here Boal, from the ex-Portuguese Brazil, exchanges with the ex-French Burkina Faso; a potential collaboration between ex-colonial subjects rather than imposition of one on the other. However, ATB learnt about Boal from the French-language editions of his books; and thus, because of his history of exile in Paris, he is easily positioned by the Burkinabé as a person from the ex-colonial centre. He could be viewed as part of the tradition of the importation of French theatrical forms at the expense of local practices. The influence of his practice on ATB could easily be placed within a 'narrative of loss', where its practice has the 'white mask, black skin' identity castigated by the classic critic of French colonialism Franz Fanon (Fanon, 1986). It is not only a response to these possible interpretations that is worth exploring but also how this relationship itself is presented by ATB. Its willingness to adopt the Boalian language of 'Forum' must be analysed within the context of the narrative that could be critical of it. In addition, the labelling of a phase of its work must be differentiated from the actual practice it seeks to categorise.

ATB encountered the work of Boal through his writing and his actual visit to Burkina in the mid-1980s. He ran a series of workshops that became part of the process whereby ATB 'adopted the denomination and borrowed certain techniques' (Duhamel and Bordet, 1994, p. 21) from his arsenal of 'theatre of the oppressed' exercises. However, in their thesis Duhamel and Bordet go on to explain that the 'sociocultural context of Burkina without doubt imposed a certain recasting of the original theory' (Duhamel and Bordet, 1994, p. 21). The exact nature of that recasting and the need to make this claim raise certain questions. Did the process of two practices meeting create something new or was the 'original' protected within the recast form? In addition, why were certain denominations (most notably the word 'Forum') used? Within the particular setting of ATB, why was it efficacious to take on the names of Boal's work and how much did the names relate to the specifics of practice? These are of course vital questions to the practice of applied theatre, both literally in examining how Boal has influenced this field, and also in the fact that this is a discussion of how a form gets changed by the context into which it is placed. Tracing the way Boal's work has changed can give insight to how theatre itself gets 'recast' when it meets the new arenas in which applied theatre works.

I want to outline here how ATB and particularly its director, Prosper Kompaoré, places Forum Theatre within an African theatre tradition. Also, how it is linked to actual practices (notably the Burkinabé Kotéba form) and how this usage must be seen within a wider system of discursive formations that are determined by factors specific to the context of Burkina Faso and postcolonial West Africa. Whereas Forum was a 'denomination' and a practice that Kompaoré wanted to align himself to on the one hand, this is confused by how he explains the recasting of it. He seeks to adopt the 'foreign' label but 'indigenise' the practice; to borrow but claim that it was ATB's already.

In an unpublished thesis on ATB, Joy Morrison makes the claim that Forum, far from being a form imported into Burkinabé theatre, in fact 'developed indigenously in Burkina Faso modelled after a traditional form of community problem solving' (Morrison, 1991, p. 5). She found it 'interesting that the same genre of theater began in Burkina Faso independently from these Brazilian activists' (Morrison, 1991, p. 6). I cannot prove the validity of this perspective, but I believe that its slightly dismissive tone ('these Brazilian activists') and use of terms such as 'same genre' and 'independently', illustrate that this is as much part of a construction of a narrative for a particular purpose, as it is a description of what really was taking place. Her argument is situated within the narrative of loss where any non-Burkinabé form is assumed to have a negative or destructive influence on local practices. It is making a claim that ATB's practice of Forum is an example of the coincidental occurrence of two forms from different locations and that therefore one cannot be criticised as an imposition on the other. This is repeated in Prosper Kompaoré's comments in the quotation above where ATB is credited as discovering Forum like the 'bourgeois gentilhomme' before it realised that 'this Brazilian' had claimed it as his own. I do not seek to undermine the claim made here, but to demonstrate that the narrative of loss influences the way this theatre is framed. These accounts are as much a response to that narrative as a description of the practice of ATB. They reveal an unspoken criticism that it is seeking to counter, but ironically by answering the critique, it also acts to accept its validity.

Although I do not wish to contradict the idea that credit for 'discovering' theatre forms is often misplaced and denies the creative activity of usually non-Western/Northern individuals and groups, I believe that the use here is contradictory. To ATB, Boal is both part of an imposed French culture (see the Molière reference on p. 110 above), and a 'traditional' African one. In much of his analysis of ATB's Forum theatre, the director Prosper Kompaoré connects it directly to local practice. He does this in general terms and specifically in comparing it to a particular Burkinabé form. His generalising perspective creates an essential Africanness where, for example, he argues that 'public participation is an essential given in our traditions' and 'the forms of dramatisation in use in our societies do not expect a clean dichotomy between actors on the one side and spectators on the other' (ATB, 1998c, p. 3). The participative heart of the practice coupled with a blurring of the division between actor and spectator make a clear link to the democratising impulse of Boal's theatre of the oppressed. However, although ATB's practice is linked to Boal, Kompaoré is drawing a direct line to a 'previous' tradition, insisting therefore that there is no corruption or loss involved in his work. ATB has direct roots in a Burkinabé/African tradition that is merely named by Boal as 'Forum'. The characteristic of African theatre with its 'impromptu involvement of the audience be it through ululation or verbal commentaries' (Byam, 1998, p. 231) is continued, not interrupted, in the practice of ATB.

Kompaoré's specific comparison comes in his link of Forum to the Burkinabé practice of Kotéba. This is a village-based form that includes speech, dancing and chanting taking place over many hours. The multiple performance forms are constructed specifically to comment on or criticise aspects of the life of a particular community or the behaviour of a particular individual. In a Kotéba event seven concentric circles of participants create a central space in which small plays or scenes are performed. These represent the faults of a villager or display the problems of a whole village. Once portrayed the action then demands that the public find a solution. Before the performance, a man enters the circle: he tells the public what scenes will happen before leaving the scene to the actors. The public can demand clarification during the action and villagers who have been criticised can intervene to defend themselves. The singers and drummers are then used to draw out the moral lessons for the community.

Clearly there are echoes of Forum in Kotéba and it is this link plus prior existence of the form that ATB is claiming. Kotéba is a form of inclusive community problem-solving that underpins the philosophy and practice of ATB as much as the specific techniques it has taken directly from Boal. However, I think it unhelpful to simplify the differences between these two forms by making one a version of the other. It is the desire to make these links in the first place that is significant for the practice of applied theatre. I think we can compare the application of Boal to the theatre-rich context of Burkina to the application of participatory or other theatre practices to non-theatrical sites. In applying theatre to these arenas, it needs to be translated to make it both understandable and meaningful in that place. It needs to forge links with comparable practices. By 'meaningful', I propose that it must develop its own theoretical markers, its own 'local' reference points, if it is to be accepted, used and take root. Boal in Burkina had to be translated and compared to Burkinabé practices for it to have resonance. Applied-theatre practice might have many of its origins in the Boal/Freire-inspired literacy campaigns in Peru,but it must build linguistic and practice links with radically different practice/ discursive formulations if it is to become truly applied in new settings.

In drawing the comparison to Kotéba ATB is making a claim to its practice having endogenous (locally derived) rather than exo-genous (externally derived) origins. The discursive use of 'Forum' is backed by the Burkinabé-rooted practice. It is clearly important for it to make this claim, partly I would contend because it is the narrative of loss that is predominant in the discourse surrounding its and other African theatre and development practice. The strength of this narrative accounts for the slight defensiveness that I believe exists in its statements about its relation to Boal (see the opening quotation). Part of the reason for this is that there is a critique of its work from within Burkina Faso. It is thus reacting to a specific reproach. The director of 'Théâtre de la Fraternité' Jean-Pierre Guingame from the Department of Arts and Sciences at the University of Ouagadougou

120

has made the claim that a Burkinabé theatre should use existing forms and respect traditional practices in theatrical representations. In an interview conducted by Joy Morrison he is said to consider 'Forum theatre an imported genre, not very suitable for Burkina Faso' (Morrison, 1991, p. 55). This is a direct critique of interculturalism, of the mixing of cultural forms, and a claim that while some practices might 'suit' Burkina, others do not. As ATB is well known nationally in Burkina as the main proponent of Forum Theatre, this cannot be anything other than a direct comment on its practice. It is this criticism that I believe frames ATB's claims to its Forum having indigenous roots, as much as the reality of the comparison. Its descriptions of practice and explanations of Forum cannot be detached from what is clearly an ongoing debate about the appropriateness of certain theatre forms within Burkina itself. The discourse of the 'narrative of loss' is thus vital and determining.

The narrative of loss

Pierre Guingame's comments can of course be included in the narrative that distrusts the mixing of cultural forms and claims that these exchanges will involve a damage or loss of the 'local'. I want to show here that although I am not dismissing this as a relevant critique of many intercultural performance events, it simplifies both how Boal was adapted by ATB and how any cultural action becomes meaningful in a particular community.

The 'narrative of loss' is not only operational within the context of Burkina Faso. It is apparent in the anxieties of applied-theatre practitioners seeking to marry creative principles to challenging contexts. Part of the motivation of writing this chapter comes from the fact that it informed my impressions of ATB when I witnessed 'Forum Theatre training courses' run by the company in 1999. I was there as the UK representative of a project overseen at first by the TIPP Centre and later by People's Palace Projects (PPP). The project was funded by Comic Relief (a UK international development agency) and included a three-year grant that supported the courses described here. The fact that I use the word 'witnessed' indicates the lack of clarity about my role during this visit. Whether I was there as manager, assessor, partner or 'witness' was not articulated sufficiently and added to the difficulty in knowing how I should be examining the work. In this moment taking the role of applied-theatre practitioner, I confused what I now see as descriptions of practice with its actual practice. I was therefore at first critical of what I saw because it did not conform to my preconceived idea of Forum Theatre. I imported my own narrative of loss, by assuming that the practice of Boal had been radically and inappropriately changed in this context. Training sessions of the regional theatre groups involved teaching them an ATB-created AIDS play and strictly taking them through an arduous rehearsal process. Workshops with young street children constantly missed the possibility for creative exploration by concentrating on the need for a final presentation. The 'tradition' that I came from and thought was followed here, was 'lost' in this intercultural meeting. Of course, this was an imposition of a notion of purity and correctness of a cultural form that was inappropriate and unhelpful in trying to understand the work of ATB.

Applied-theatre practice in the context of criminal-justice agencies had already contorted Boal's arsenal of theatre of the oppressed to a shape that to many was not a recognisable relative of the original. I had permitted this in my own practice, but in witnessing this Burkinabé example of theatre application, I had yearned for an assumed original. Clearly, ATB had developed a highly structured and powerful practice within its context, which was then articulated and explained to different audiences. Its position in relation to the development agency audience in Burkina was certainly stronger than any prison theatre practitioners in the UK were to criminal-justice institutions. Its 'performance' therefore in this context made it an important 'player' in this arena. Although it adopted the term 'Forum', claiming that it was compatible with its practice, critics such as Guingame had mistakenly taken this as a wholesale practical adoption rather than a helpful discursive act. Its practice had taken many Boalian techniques and approaches but in a way that was far more complicated than replication or imposition. The Beninoise philosopher Pauline Hountonji has commented that 'the decisive encounter is not between Africa as a whole and Europe as a whole' (quoted by Jeyifo, 1996, p. 153). Here it is clear that 'the decisive encounter' is not between ATB as a whole and Boal as a whole. There is no uni-directional, wholesale adoption or imposition from one place to another. Ironically, Guingame and I, while coming from different points of view, were creating a similar simplistic reading of the encounter. Both of us saw a traditional form under threat from a perceived new practice. For me Forum was damaged in the context of ATB's theatre, for him Burkinabé's theatre was compromised by the influence of Forum. I now believe that the encounter with Boal involved neither the 'loss' of that form within a new context, nor did it involve the impoverishment of Burkinabé theatre due to the power of the external. The interaction – that decisive encounter – was far more complex, rich and dynamic. To respect that complexity, the analysis must be wary of those interpretations that are inflected with the anxieties of the 'narrative of loss' and must start to articulate a difficult, multi-layered 'narrative of gains'.

In terms of applied theatre this illustrates the danger of relating theatre practice within new sites or institutions as one of the simple struggle to avoid compromise and hold on to an 'artistic integrity'. All forms of theatre practice are already minutely tied into the histories, traditions and philosophies in which they are situated. They have already adapted, changed and applied themselves to a context. They were never 'pure'; they were always 'compromised'. They were already the result of many shifting and particular 'encounters' within and between practices in their own settings. Application to a new arena therefore should not lament additional transformations. As with interculturalism, any shift of a cultural practice into a new place will be implicated in complex relations of power and control (see Bharucha, 1990). However, this often forgets that the art form being transferred is already situated and developed within its own systems of authority. It is not a free-floating practice unsullied by the world of unequal exchange, but a vitally determined, 'compromised' and context-battered practice entering a place that is similarly constructed. I am not denying inequalities of power, but insisting that those inequalities operate in diverse, multi-directional and disparate ways. Forum was no pure form adopted by or imposed upon ATB. It was already a result of complex interactions, exchanges and encounters entering, in Burkina Faso, a new realm with a practice that was already multiple and complex. The 'decisive encounter' for applied theatre therefore is never between the art form as a whole and the institution or community as a whole.

An imposing project

Since 1998, I had been involved in a project with ATB developing a Forum Theatre training programme for regional theatre companies. The aim of this initiative was to train a company from every region of Burkina Faso in Forum Theatre. These companies would then use their skills to create plays to tackle local development issues in their own particular areas. The commentary provided in this chapter has been formed through this relationship and the dilemmas that have arisen because of it. One of the objectives of this project has been to ensure for these groups that 'the instrument of development will no longer come from outside and misrepresent at times local realities, but [...] will be the result of an internal dynamic belonging to that community' (SAEC, 1998, p. 30). This mission of course fits neatly into the problems already outlined above. Although I am comfortable with the rhetoric of communities representing their own realities, it does not acknowledge that the instrument to enable their self-development is imported from ATB and a Brazilian 'gentilhomme'. Although this importation is rarely as simple as an imposition, there is a paradoxical relation between the local and the external in the construction of this project.

This paradox can be further illustrated by the project's administrative and financial structure. It was facilitated by money that was granted by a UK donor (Comic Relief) and managed through charities which because of the regulations of that donor, had to be based in the UK. The TIPP Centre and later PPP had to control the money, which was then directed to ATB. The Burkinabé company wrote the project in French, which we then translated both into English and into the precise requirements of Comic Relief's application forms. One of the requirements of their grants was that the money was only given on the basis that there was a 'partnership' with a 'local' delivery organisation. Whereas often the UK charity would be the controlling larger partner in such a programme, here ATB was a considerably larger organisation than the smaller-scale operations of TIPP and PPP. The flow of the money still played a determining factor, but the simplistic formulation of the externally powerful determining local practices was made more complex by the relative size and age of the organisations. While Comic Relief demanded Burkinabé control of project implementation, it still insisted the money was managed through the UK. Operational control was devolved as a matter of principle, whereas financial control was maintained. Whereas the 'external' Boalian theatre insists on local control, Comic Relief's demand for 'local control' was partial. Interestingly, in its assessment of the first drafts of the application for this project, it emphasised that the theatre created must be locally generated and not be imported from elsewhere. It insisted (imposed?) that the work was created through 'the internal dynamic belonging to that community'. The external funding agency and the charities that administered the grants thus both sought to control and devolve control: to impose and insist on no imposition. These paradoxes undermine the simplicity of binaries such as the external and the internal, the outsider and the insider and will be returned to later in the chapter. The fact that in the structure of the project there were no straightforward divisions illustrates the importance of avoiding the easy readings of imposition or 'loss'.

A Burkinabé Forum: an applied theatre in practice

So, what was this Forum Theatre in Burkina? What was the practice that had the denomination 'forum' but a confused relation to the work of Boal? The next section of the chapter will examine how ATB manages the relationship between different audiences, agencies and funding bodies mentioned above. In particular it aims to explore how ATB describes its Forum work, how the context of Burkina Faso has impacted on that practice, and how it differed from my expectations of Forum Theatre.

Since the Forum phase of its work started in 1984, ATB has created plays on an impressive range of development issues. As well as those mentioned above, it has been involved in campaigns linked to mother and child health; environmental problems and land management; peace and social justice; the schooling of girls and female excision (circumcision). The different themes are developed in a system that involves the presentation of an 'anti-model' scene to a community who are in turn encouraged to intervene to change the particular situation. In the words of Boal, 'theatre must always present doubt and not certainty, must always be an *anti-model* not a *model'* (Boal, 1992, p. 232). The Forum structure is described by Prosper Kompaoré (Morrison, 1991, p. 69) using the exact terms of Boal (Boal, 1992, p. 232). On reading, therefore, it is hard at first to see how it 'has been adapted by Burkina Faso' (Morrison, 1991, p. 69). Although my experience of seeing Forum Theatre training in Burkina made me question ATB's practice, actual visits to Forum presentations in villages and during the International Festival have also shown this basic similarity. The play ('anti-model') is performed, there is a Joker character to introduce the Forum and there are interventions from the audience to 'solve' the problem. It must be stated that my experience of these events reinforces the power of Forum theatre to generate participative community-led dialogue. In ATB-supported productions I have seen thousands of people crowd around an open-air space to watch performances, in which they appear completely engaged. The vision of women performing with their

126

babies still tied to their backs, and the hoes that mark out t
of dried-out land hacking at the real dried out dirt of
space', make these powerful moments vitally conne
audience and its members' lives. Forum seems very 'true
although at the same time completely specific to this setting. Of
course, that specificity is my reading and it is hard to judge how the
huge audience view the relevance of the form. Evaluations of ATB
presentations have interviewed audience members but these tend to
ask about the issues and people's memory of them, rather than the
impact of the Forum itself (see for example 'L'Étude d'impact du
theatre-forum sur le developpement', Société Africaine d'Étude et
Conseils, 1998).

However there are differences in the structure of the Forums and
it is these that I want to concentrate on here. Whereas these changes
are manifested in a variety of ways, I believe they originate from this
theatre's relationship to the context of Burkina and to an
understanding of the concept of 'development' specifically. In much
of its literature and on a huge sign that is hung outside its base in
Ouagadougou, ATB proclaims that it practices 'theatre at the service
of development'. Although the director has said, 'we must be master
of what we put in the word development' (Thompson, 1999b, p. 110),
indicating a desire to take control of the discourse, this clearly places
theatre in a subordinate role to the context. Theatre is the servant to
the needs to the situation. *Application* in this setting therefore means
the close adaptation to the requirements of 'development', and that
agenda is negotiated between the different interests (particularly
governmental and the international agencies) who have the power to
'put in the word'. In Burkina Faso, ATB places itself at the service of
the various agencies involved in development (including the demands
of Comic Relief relayed through TIPP/PPP and eventually myself).
Although the imperative of financial survival has a part to play, it
would be unfair to criticise ATB for this. The company is judged to
see if its work is 'an exact translation of the commissioning
institution' (SAEC, 1998, p. 7) but it does not view this as restrictive
or exact. Although in this context applied theatre becomes the
subordination of the theatre to the social function determined by
particular agencies, this relationship is welcomed by ATB. In the

Duhamel and Bordet study, company members describe how the group starts with a theme that is 'proposed by a partner or chosen by the troop itself, but always imposed by its urgency in the social context of the country' (Duhamel and Bordet, 1994, p. 43). ATB relishes this imposition and sees no contradiction between the needs of development partners, itself or the country. Forum Theatre in this formulation becomes a means of communication which aims to 'carry information to a specific population which is above all clear, precise and well structured' (SAEC, 1998, p. 7). The shift from the logic of Boal here is that the community does not set the agenda but that agenda is established before the encounter. This is similar to a tendency within prison theatre that I criticised in the introduction. In addition, the work of Forum is simplified to the transmission or 'carrying' of information rather than a means to enter a dialogue. An example of this process happened in 1995 when ATB was commissioned by the National Office of Water and Purification to support its campaigns. The office reported to ATB that people blamed its projects for causing stomach upsets. In addition, there was a fear expressed that children would fall down newly dug latrines. The job of ATB would be to 'explain' the purification projects so that the communities understood their intentions. ATB 'at the service of development' responded to this need.

This emphasis has also led to a very direct change in the way a Forum event proceeds. Whereas the basic format, as I say above, is the same, there is a third stage which is certainly a 'Burkinabé' adaptation (this is of course not to say that this change has not happened elsewhere). In its twentieth-anniversary leaflet it explains the three stages of Forum as first the anti-model, second the interventions and third 'a large debate [...] with the aim to expand the information and to clarify aspects not sufficiently explained' (ATB 1998a, p. 3). This debate is also referred to as the 'specialist' section, where the development agency or ATB itself brings an informed person so that the audience's questions 'receive authoritative responses' (Morrison, 1991, p. 69). In an internal evaluation of the Forum Theatre training project undertaken for PPP by Joel Anderson, it was reported that 'the "specialistes" section of the forum was seen very positively'. The spectators 'respect and trust the information they

128

receive in this section' (Anderson, 2000, p. 10). It would be easy to dismiss these 'adaptations' as counter to some of the accepted 'rules' of modern development practice (see for example Chambers, 1997; Munck and O'Hearn, 1999). The outside expert is given prominence over locally generated knowledge. The community receive development information, and its fears are a problem to be overcome rather than an anxiety that is to be acknowledged or legitimised. At first glance, the dialogic theatre of Boal seems to be replaced by the didactic theatre of the message, a theatre practice where if the information is not 'clear' enough the specialist will be there to clarify people's doubts. This seems to be a major break from the doubt-inspiring theatre of the anti-model. A break that perhaps harks back to my anti-Poll-Tax days?

However, I believe these concerns, although relevant, obscure a more complicated relation between ATB's practice, Boal and the demands of the commissioning institutions. Whereas clearly the use of theatre as message carrier is part of the history and development of an applied theatre (see Plastow, 1998; Mooneeram, 1999), I have already argued that we should attempt a break from this didactic past to prioritise a transitive or dialogic practice. Here it appears that the practice of ATB is very much caught within a propagandist format. It uses its plays to 'carry' messages to the information-poor villages of Burkina. I believe now, however, that although this is a legitimate line of argument, it in fact draws one into a 'narrative of loss' that then relates more to the dynamics of that narrative than to the peculiarities of the Burkina situation. My concern to protect an imagined Boalian purity when I first engaged with ATB's practice was my 'narrative of loss' being imposed on the dynamic of a rich and extremely unforgiving applied-theatre arena. Reading 'loss' says more about the reader's anxiety in relation to the art of applying theatre than the practice that is being criticised. I have seen Boal's work radically translated in the context of prison theatre so that it creates a dialogue with that arena. To do this certain discursive formulations and arena-specific practice principles became incorporated into the theatre so that it was *meaningful* in that setting. As I have stated above, this is not a loss of something pure but a reworking of a form that is already the product of engagements with and translations within varied areas

129

of social life. ATB is 'true' to the work of Boal and to applied theatre by maintaining the close and responsive relation with its context. A nurse 'specialist' answering questions on family planning in a village after a play is an intelligent addition that validates the questions of the audience rather than imposing an expertise. It respects doubt by providing a source of information that affirms their desire for clarification. Dismissing the elements of didacticism within ATB's practice denies what Anderson reported was the 'respect and trust' the audience showed for these aspects of the events. Its work of course should be questioned, but the narrative of loss, by judging against a standard, only helps close and reject, rather than opening a practice for understanding or enquiry.

The shifts discussed at the beginning of the book, from the didactic, to the bleary-eyed, to the full rehabilitation translation, to the retracing of principles, becomes further complicated in the example of ATB. Its 'translation' as an act of applying theatre refigured elements of didacticism and again raised questions about 'principles'. Applying theatre demands flexibility in use of theatre forms in a search for their relevance in the arenas of application. Therefore can we ever insist on a notion of applied-theatre principles without getting caught in a 'narrative of loss' that denies the dynamic of the translation of theatre to a new context? Does the claim to principle (for example, the importance of dialogic forms) inevitably involve an act of imposition that we are perhaps trying to avoid 'in principle'? Does this repeat the paradox of the funding agency imposing local control? This is a version of the dance between clarity and confusion that rather than be resolved is often what provides a creative impetus behind applied-theatre work. It is the 'balancing act' that is central to many questions in this book, and will be returned to in further detail in the final chapter.

A consensual development?

ATB's Forum Theatre is developed in a context that has both a more consensual vision of development and a more complicated view of the divisions within the communities in which it works. What is referred to above as the 'urgency in the social context of the country' cannot be minimised in understanding how ATB frames and develops its practice. The extreme poverty, high levels of illiteracy and desperate problems with land management in the north of the country create a situation where social problems are often viewed as obvious and beyond debate. In his opening speech to the International Festival for Theatre for Development the Minister for Communication and Culture Mahamoudou Ouedraogo thanked artists for 'carrying their stone in the national construction project' (ATB, 1998c, p. 2). Although it is clearly in this politician's interest to create a picture of a unified national project of construction, that vision does have a strong impact on the way ATB both perceives and generates its work. My meetings and work with ATB artists were marked by their enthusiasm for 'building' their country, which in most cases meant meeting some of their people's very basic needs. If their theatre was to be 'at the service of development', that practice had to be affected by what was 'put in' the word by the Burkina Faso context. Although the whole ATB team would be engaged in defining the parameters for what 'development' meant, it would be futile to assume it could ever have complete control. In all examples of applied theatre we engage with discursive practices established for the contexts in which we work, over which we will struggle to have influence. To have any hope of being master of the meaning, we have to enter the debate – we have to practice within those structures. By engaging in development theatre within a country that has a dominant discourse of national consensual construction, ATB more easily becomes incorporated into a 'theatre of reconstruction' rather than a 'theatre for struggle' (Kerr, 1999, p. 79). Within this context, following agendas that are preset for it becomes more understandable. ATB does not see a clear-cut difference between the agenda of the government, its beliefs on what are the pressing issues, the needs of the non-governmental agencies and the demands of the communities in which it works. Although this is not to state that differences do not exist, it does illustrate that theatre application in this context is determined very heavily by these boundaries.

This vision of consensus is complicated however by a practice that implicitly recognises that the impoverished villages and urban communities in which ATB works are not places of total harmony. It is a vast simplification if the internal village view is reified as the local and good and the external, 'outside' expertise is the imposition of control and therefore bad. Boal's theatre, although explicitly aiming to be dynamically responsive to the community, can be unfairly caricatured as promoting total autonomy of the community and a version of this simple dichotomy. Simple divisions between the oppressed and the oppressors are rarely the appropriate script for development problems. This is true in the majority of social settings, and is certainly the case in rural Burkina Faso. The picture of older village members resisting the mission to eradicate female circumcision, brought from the outside but supported by younger women in the community, disturbs neat boundaries between endogenous and exogenous development. It makes a theatre that prioritises a public forum driven by a common analysis of the problem by a unified oppressed group harder to insist upon. The innovation of creating low stone walls in contours in the land to help prevent soil erosion and aid water retention, is a practice encouraged in the drought-affected, Sahel-encroached regions of the north of Burkina. This technique is brought from the outside and disliked by certain community members anxious about change. Again, to insist that the community must set the agenda as a development or applied-theatre principle denies it the right to benefit from appropriate technological developments from outside its knowledge base. Villages in Burkina are divided along lines of age, gender, income, social position, employment and education, leading to little consensus as to which problems should be prioritised, let alone how to solve them. ATB's theatre has been carved by and within these boundaries, and cannot be judged by principles created in response to other problematic situations.

Every circumstance to which a theatre project is applied will similarly make its own demands for the adaptations of practice. Principles of how to implement a workshop or a theatre programme are always the product of previous negotiations, and although they might guide a new encounter, they can never dictate how it should develop. To simplistically extract the method from the specifics of the moment in which it was formed, either to reform it elsewhere or criticise it, misses the 'applied' part of applied theatre. Understanding applied theatre requires an examination of how a context affects, makes demands upon or constrains at the same time as exploring how that practice adapts to or resists these determining factors. Claims to a 'true theatre for development' (Plastow, 1998, p. 103) or an 'ideal' applied-theatre practice, imply that the work exists beyond or above the actual moments in which it happens. Although, as I have already noted, I am not dismissing ideals or principles outright, we need to remember who has the power to construct these models and be aware how easily they can be used as the external critical club to attack the practice that is carved in the hardest and most testing of settings. The pragmatics of ensuring the survival of theatre on the ground is often more impressive than the clean models constructed within the academies.

Doing it wrong – the dangers of orthodoxy

> ATB has practised forum theatre in *a relatively orthodox way* since 1983, creating on average 3 campaigns of sensibilisation each year. (Duhamel and Bordet, 1994, p. 22; italics added)

Insisting on orthodoxy implies that the theatre form has a universal structure unresponsive to changes in environment, and vitally it suggests that it is not a product of some particular time and place. I agree with Julie Stone Peters in her criticism of 'those who insist on the radicality of difference [who] feel uncomfortable with the mixing of cultures and forms' (Peters, 1995, p. 207). Whereas she is discussing intercultural performance (and of course the narrative of loss), I am commenting on similar 'mixing' in applications of theatre. Although there are many examples of 'orthodox' performance forms that appear static and permanent, a theatre practice in fact is always a product of 'the mixing of cultures and forms' at some stage of its development. Boal himself admits that his theatre was created in this type of process over many years;

> I did not invent Theatre of the Oppressed by myself, in my house, nor did I receive it as tablets of stone from God: it was in the interaction with popular audiences that TO was born, little by little. It did not come to me ready and finished: it created itself by a process of exchange. (Boal, 2001, p. 339)

Duhamel and Bordet's claim that ATB is 'orthodox' in its use of Forum is therefore unnecessary. In fact ATB is fairly confident in how the particularities of Burkina have meant that the inspiration that undoubtedly has come from Boal has been changed and reformed. Its theatre is a rich mix of Burkinabé performance, the French colonial and of other African and of course Boalian forms that has coalesced and thrived in the context of Burkina. To return to Stone Peters, 'an insistence on authenticity (an insistence on orthodoxy) shows little recognition of the conditions of theatre, or [...] of cultural pluralism' (Peters, 1995, pp. 207–8). This is not to minimise the fact that the history of colonialism in Burkina has erased, challenged or imposed certain forms. It does however affirm ATB as an active generator of theatre within this history. It has been producing and responding to these circumstances and has not been a passive victim of them.

Reading the practice of ATB as either the dilution of orthodoxy or the imposition of an alternative orthodoxy is part of the narrative that I have been referring to throughout this chapter. Although I argue above for a 'recognition of the conditions of theatre' and an acknowledgement that ATB practice is in fact an example of rich 'cultural pluralism', I must not dismiss the fact that I too 'felt uncomfortable' when I first witnessed its work. The training in Forum Theatre did not use the techniques with which I was familiar. It prioritised scripts in a way that I felt was inappropriate, it insisted on a directorial control in a stricter way than I assumed necessary; it appeared more didactic

134

than transitive. The challenge this poses is that while I can argue against orthodoxy, I clearly do hold, however implicitly, certain ideas about 'correct ways of working'. I too have formed a 'clean model' within my academic space. This submerged sense of orthodoxy was only revealed when its rules were transgressed in the moment of witnessing workshops in Ouagadougou. What I call principles above, were made visible as they were encroached on by the practice. Although it might be unfashionable to acknowledge it, I had an affective response of disapproval during this training event. This chapter is part of a challenge to that view, but the initial reaction should not be erased by my rational counter to it. Again, a 'balancing act' is encountered. My gut response raises the question of when should we dismiss our universalising principles as a lack of recognition of 'the conditions of theatre', and when should we hold onto them as appropriate guides to practice? This experience hinted at an internally held limit to my belief that 'values are hard-won and contingent' (Schechner, 2002, p. 1). That is a limit that is more directly reached in the final example of practice in the ethics debate outlined in chapter five. In this example towards the end of the book, the 'balancing act' was tipped in a different direction, away from the relativism that is asserted here.

The 'Specialistes' – theatre carries an unpredictable message

I want to return to one particular challenge to 'orthodoxy' that the example of ATB provides in order to elaborate further my doubts and questions about its influence. One of the major parts of the narrative of loss that I at first imposed on the practice of ATB was an assumption that the transitive ideal of Boal's theatre was weakened by the presence of the 'specialistes'. If the priority of development education has shifted to trusting the knowledge of the community, hearing members' opinions and learning from them, how could we privilege the expert information-giver? I held onto the strong belief that Forum Theatre involved the community setting its own agenda. If it was not doing this, it was not (and should not be called?) 'Forum'. Giving information or using theatre to deliver a message was what Osita Okagbu refers to as the 'consumption vision' of theatre for development rather than the liberatory (Okagbu, 1998, p. 24). I have already mentioned the 'respect and trust' that villagers had for these moments and therefore this critique is challenged by the response to the practice. However, further inspection of ATB's work also demonstrates that even when it articulates what appears to be a 'consumptionist' plan, its practice rarely exists neatly within this frame. As I have outlined above, moments such as the nurse specialist giving information cannot be so easily dismissed. In fact, more often ATB moves beyond the simplicity of these categories and thus both confuses and reframes 'principles' in the practice of Applied Theatre.

There has been a strong criticism of the information-giving direction of theatre for development. Frances Harding sees the practice as 'increasingly blocked by this direct cause-analysis-action paradigm' (Harding, 1998, p. 5). For Okagbu the impact of this work is dismissed as merely creating 'ripples in the pond of the oppressed which returns to relative calm when the buzz or excitement of the ripples are gone' (Okagbu, 1998, p. 32). These comments do offer a valuable critique of the limited and mechanistic ways of describing or explaining theatre for development (which are prominent in the analyses of ATB's work that I have cited here – see Morrison, 1991 and SAEC, 1998). However, I think ATB shows that even with a very pronounced 'cause-analysis-action' paradigm, the actual events it creates rarely can be contained within this simple progression. This is also hinted at in Jane Plastow's analysis of the state-sponsored agit-prop performances in post-revolutionary Ethiopia. Although she is highly critical of their content she adds as an aside that 'many youths enjoyed for the first time being involved in making drama without apparently worrying too much about the content' (Plastow, 1998, p. 103). The point to emphasise is that within information-giving or propaganda theatre, the impact cannot be solely judged in terms of the efficacy of the passing of ideas. There is an affective response to both witnessing and participating in theatre that should be a significant, not

136

marginal, part of the enquiry. The enjoyment of those young people is a crucial ingredient to the potential of theatre in these contexts, not an insignificant extra. Okagbu's ripples are an unpredictable force than should not be ignored because they are only transitory. They are part of the 'temporary sensitising moment' that was referred to in the discussions of prison-theatre work in chapter two. They are those 'marking moments' that, even though they may fade, may also lead to unexpected waves emerging in other places or times. Dismissing the ripples implies an optimistic vision of a greater untapped potential of theatre that I would argue is rarely fully explained.

The unpredictable outcomes of an explicitly 'information-giving' practice of theatre can be seen in many examples of ATB's work. In the 'Forums' run by ATB or its regional groups, the event itself becomes an energetic and vital moment in the life of the community. The presence of hundreds and sometimes thousands of people at a performance is an extraordinary moment, the effect of which cannot be reduced to the nature of the message or information passed. One interviewee in the SAEC evaluation spoke of his inspiration to mobilise young people to build a school after seeing a Forum performance. The external – exogenous – performance provoked an act of endogenous development that was not directly related to the subject matter of the play. This is a clear echo of the ex-prisoner who decided to become a nursery nurse discussed in chapter two. The buzz or the ripples had affected this young person, proving the capacity of Forum 'to arouse more ideas than it announces' (SAEC, 1998, p. 14). So my feeling of discomfort at the unorthodox style of ATB's use of Forum, and Guingame's criticism of Forum as an imposition of an external inappropriate theatre form, are countered here by a young man who found an apparently unconnected inspiration in the performance. While I was reading 'unorthodox', and others the inequalities of intercultural 'exchange', the event in fact went beyond what it 'announced'.

Whatever the explicit intent of a range of ATB's work, the company has found that it is the unpredictable that is often the most notable. Although the external agency might commission it to develop a play on, for example, the theme of AIDS, the moment of performance will ensure that the transmission or consumption of that message is rarely straightforward. It will always 'arouse more'. The SAEC evaluation notes this when it speaks of the performance allowing for 'the sensibilisation of the administrator and the administered by putting them face to face' (SAEC, 1998, p. 13). Although the objective is to pass information, it never occurs as a simple one-way transmission. A transitive interaction seems to be forced by the moment. The necessity of 'face to face' encounters means that an exchange will happen. The webs of connections between audience and actors are created in a live moment, built by the action of the event. The plays themselves have the power to 'enable the two parties to interrogate their objectives and their roles' and 'ATB can open the eyes of those in charge to the limits of their project' (Duhamel and Bordet, 1994, p. 46). Discovering the limits of a project demonstrates that by using theatre a response will be elicited however didactic the performance might have seemed. So the contradiction found in ATB's simultaneous use of terminology borrowed from Boal while following strict commissions to pass on information is dissipated by the realities of the actual practice, which constantly shifts between these two and in addition creates effect beyond what is intended.

This ability to create learning in unpredictable ways and have impact outside or surplus to set objectives is crucial for understanding and discussing applied theatre. The explicit intent of practice should never be viewed as the same as the outcome. Just because a project announces itself as a health education play does not mean automatically that an audience member will attend a clinic. They could be inspired to build a school. A statement on practice by a company, a decision to be commissioned or cooperate with an external agency, will never contain the impact of that practice. For these reasons a company cannot be criticised from the perspective of how it discusses or describes its work alone. It will never be telling the full story of the impact of the work. The meeting of theatre and areas of application will create unpredictable moments, ripples or affective responses that are perhaps minute or sometimes powerful but always worthy of attention. Hoping for a purity of intent, orthodoxy of form and predictability of outcome seems to imply that there can be a singular effect. Although we might still be critical of, for example, government-sponsored agitprop, we should not let this minimise the potentially transformative impact of the participation of the young people in the moment of the project. We need to take a lead from the youth who 'enjoyed making drama' and start to analyse that enjoyment, rather than only 'worrying' about the unsavoury content.

Blurring Dichotomies

One problem in holding onto orthodoxy is that it tends to create dichotomous categories for the analysis of practice. For example, in relying on an ideal of Boalian theatre in my first meeting with ATB, I created an over-simple division between theatre than poses problems and a didactic or (to borrow from Freire) 'banking' theatre that passes information. On the one hand there was (in the rhetoric of the funding application completed to fulfil the demands of Comic Relief) a fully participative theatre that had its agenda set by the community, and on the other there was a theatre that sought to educate the uneducated, prioritising the expertise of the outsider. This dichotomy was inspired by my hidden orthodoxy, the clarity required in international funding schemes and from the assumption that the word 'Forum' in ATB promotional materials neatly corresponded to a generalised under-standing of that practice. These determining factors denied the obvious shifts that happen in intercultural translations of theatre. They also denied the fact that in applied-theatre work in the UK practice had shifted and metamorphosed from Boalian and many other sources under the influence and demands of the different criminal-justice or other agencies.

This dichotomy is of course unhelpful, and certainly shown to be false in the work of ATB. The very structure of the Comic Relief-funded project confused many development dichotomies, including this one. The divisions between endogenous versus exogenous projects, top down versus bottom up, or insider against outsider development, are never clear in practice. In this initiative funded by an international agency (who insisted on local operational control of the project), ATB was bringing theatre skills to teach regional theatre groups how to do 'Forum' plays, so that those groups could go back to their local communities to do performances that tackled their own issues. There was a didactic element to the training, but it was coupled with a desire to see locally based use of Forum Theatre. ATB had an agenda, but it was to develop the skills of other groups so that they could themselves set the agenda. There were always shades of outsider-ness (PPP were an international outsider to Burkina Faso, ATB members were urban outsiders to the villagers, the local theatre groups were outsider artists within their own communities), and there were degrees of insider-ness (ATB actors were Mooré speakers, government agents were also villagers, villagers changed the performances). ATB's theatre in fact is translated between these different positions, existing only as evidence of how they are fluid rather than fixed. A vision of correct practice permits these over-neat divisions to be categories into which the practice is forced, and this does not aid the explanation of the moment.

The condom

To illustrate briefly how a dichotomy can both be blurred by ATB's practice and how it is an unhelpful explanatory tool, I want to discuss one small moment from a major play 'Sid Sida' created by ATB in 1999. This tale of the life of a young woman Tené who contracts HIV from a boyfriend and then is gradually ostracised by her family and community, was played both by ATB and the regional groups in hundreds of locations during 1999 and 2000. One of the most talked-about moments in the play was when an actor playing a doctor demonstrated how to use a condom by placing it on a banana. The interviews conducted by Joel Anderson from PPP during 1999 with audience members frequently returned to this moment. Although there were interventions taken during this play, as an 'orthodox' forum

140

would expect, it was this clearly didactic information-passing moment that seemed to impress most. The image seemed to be easily recalled and was therefore clearly fixed in memory. If the dichotomy of didactic versus transitive were used to judge this moment, it would fall within the former and potentially be dismissed by many commentators on theatre and development. A message is passed to the audience which it is invited to accept. However, the impact of this moment implies that the act of observing can never be relegated to mere passive 'banking' education. The act of witnessing the doctor demonstrating the condom had engaged the audience. It had significance in the moment for those present. It had been remembered and enthusiastically recalled, even though it was the 'simple' passing of a message. Information was not absorbed by the empty vessels that are implied by Freire's term 'banking' education (Freire, 1970, p. 52), but memorised by engaged, active and thinking people. It 'marked' to use the language of the first chapter. Information therefore can become a query in a person's mind even if it is framed as fact. How that 'fact' translates can only be determined by the reality of the live moment. It cannot be predetermined precisely. This requires a much deeper understanding of the cultural practices and 'marking histories' of the audience rather than a detailed analysis of the cultural origins of the theatre practice alone. The dichotomy of the transitive versus the didactic thus becomes an unhelpful interpretative device because in this instance, it erased the specificity of the moment. The potential for a powerful engagement with theatre practice therefore needs to be judged at the point of its execution and should be wary of relying in a fixed way on pre-existing models. This is, perhaps, another claim that as an initial research strategy 'bewilderment' is more productive than the potentially reductive effect of departing from a position of clarity.

Applied theatre and interculturalism

Applied Theatre learns from intercultural performance debates not only in the analysis of the development of theatre form. It should not be reduced only to tracing the Boalian roots or the aspects of traditional Burkinabé performance that lurk under the skin of an ATB performance event. Biodun Jeyifo's question as to '*which* African or European sources and influences do we find operative and combined in any given African theatrical expression' (Jeyifo, 1996, p. 157) certainly offers a more nuanced approach to analysis, avoiding the simplicity of seeing African theatre practice as one of imposition of the colonial on the local. It avoids the sense of powerlessness and inevitability evident in the 'narrative of loss'. However, applied theatre needs to move beyond the analysis of the theatre practice itself and ask which other *non-theatrical* sources do we find 'operative and combined' in the work. The interaction of cultures is thus not only between different theatre forms leading to syntheses in theatre practice, but also between theatre practice and the new arena – the development situation, the prison, the school, the hospital and so forth. These too are zones of cultural practice that interact with theatre to create an interculturalism of very different disciplines. The complexity of that interaction needs to be understood in the moment of the meeting. The cultural norms, histories, discursive practices and assumptions that are continually negotiated within a Burkinabé village meet the contextually specific practice of ATB to create a rich intercultural/interdisciplinary event.

It is because applied theatre is an intentional engagement of different disciplines that the link to intercultural performance is so strong. The infusion, exchange or synthesis between different forms that might be tried on stage is a related process to the deliberate mixing and juxtapositions that occur in applied theatre. The debates within interculturalism, specifically the problems of Zarrilli's 'narrative of loss', can thus become useful indicators for the stresses within the practice of applied theatre. The problems of searching for origins, insisting on orthodoxy or mistaking appropriation for fair exchange become relevant not just between theatre practitioners from different traditions but in meetings between development agencies, prison psychologists, teachers, health professionals and theatre makers.

Conclusion: audience? Moi?

ATB's theatre and the way it explains and promotes it in its various publications, is created as a response to the variety of demands it receives within its specific context. The denomination 'Forum' is used because it is both a partial description of what it seeks to practice but also because it is a performance to the international audience of theatre for development funders and practitioners. I mistakenly took a result of theatre application – an intercultural effect of the demands of international funders meeting the practice of ATB – to be a description of theatre practice. The use of the term was thus a facilitating performance, not dishonest, but part of the pragmatics of applied theatre. Clearly, it related to ATB's interactive theatre events, which did follow many of the techniques that I understood to be involved in Forum Theatre. However, it was a term that was an explanatory tool rather than a controlling category. As I hope I have showed here, even when 'operative and combined' in ATB plays, the specificity of the Burkina Faso setting still managed to slip the work from its restrictions and ensure that each performance 'aroused more than it announced'.

In describing its shift to the current Forum Theatre phase, the ATB 20th anniversary leaflet explicitly recognises that Forum was a discursive shift. It states that it 'decided to adopt the denomination forum theatre to describe the performances that it proposed from now on to create in collaboration with partners who it would approach or who solicited it' (ATB, 1998a). That 'adoption' was a key applied-theatre moment. Although I do not claim that this discursive turn had no impact on practice, it is quite wrong to criticise this action as a loss of an original Burkinabé theatre or the imposition of a Brazilian one. It was the synthesis of two arenas, producing a denomination that had a complex relationship to the actual performance practice that it described. In meeting ATB, I had assumed that I understood the style of theatre that it practised. What I came to realise was that I was one part of the arena (the representative of PPP in turn linked to the finances of Comic Relief) to which it was promoting its work. It adopted the word 'Forum' to make its theatre understandable to people like me. Having spent a number of years describing my theatre work to make it intelligible to non-theatre audiences, here were a theatre group that were now describing its theatre work to make it intelligible to the non-Burkinabé theatre world. In the project that the TIPP Centre and PPP have been involved, we were all part of another zone of cultural practice into which ATB was appropriately and deliberately applying or explaining its theatre. The initial concerns, misreading and anxieties over the practice were a product of being part of an arena to which ATB's theatre was being described. I was an audience to which it performed.

ATB provides an excellent and complex example of theatre applied to a very difficult situation. It has managed to sustain its work for over 20 years in one of the world's poorest countries. It has two theatres, runs a biennial international festival, performs issue-based plays across its country and has now trained theatre companies from almost all of the country's forty-five districts. The work is sustained by the practice meeting the needs of those that have commissioned it, fulfilling the various reporting and documenting procedures of the international 'partners' and consistently being welcomed by villages in which it works. The practice is also sustained by the company's eloquent advocacy for it within the local and international development community. It is wrong to criticise this as a compromise, appropriation or 'loss'. First, the actual performance of its plays will always have impact beyond their articulated functions. ATB's practice cannot be dismissed because of the apparent narrowness of a particular funder demand or criticised for what it writes about its work. Second, the successful forging of a theatre practice within the demands and restrictions of a particular setting should be congratulated rather than immediately made the subject of censure.

144

ATB's continued existence in the tough and economically severe setting of Ouagadougou demonstrates the strength of its applied theatre. Accessing Comic Relief funds in London from the centre of Burkina Faso demonstrates an ingenuity that must be admired as well as questioned. ATB offers a narrative of a necessarily pragmatic yet creative struggle for making theatre work for its very demanding context.

In applied theatre we accept that all arenas place difficult boundaries onto practice. It is the negotiation and innovation within what might seem an impossible situation that makes it so interesting and challenging. The fact that the most problematic spaces or disciplines are opened as sites in which theatre can battle to have a presence, shows an idealistic glint behind what is often the pragmatic exterior. Applied theatre thrives on the barriers, the compromises, the problems, the delays, the setbacks, and the restrictions. These are what make the practice, not what breaks it. Some might need comfort, pretend integrity, complain of loss, but we should welcome the fraught, dirty and difficult nature of applying theatre. And we should welcome the theatre companies, the ATBs, who conjure the work in that heat and dust.

Chapter Four
Theatre action research: a democracy of the ground

It invites: it belongs to all and is costless, familiar, fun and easy to alter [...] paper is private; the ground is public. Paper empowers those that hold the pen; the ground empowers those who are weak, marginalised and illiterate. There is a democracy of the ground. (Chambers, 1997, p. 152)

A person who rides a donkey does not know the ground is hot. (Proverb from Bawku West region of Ghana in Goyder, Davies, and Williamson, 1998, p. 31)

We make the road by walking. (Horton and Freire, 1990)

This chapter moves from the specifics of past practice to an advocacy of possible practice. It turns from analysing the particular to outlining a different way of understanding applied-theatre projects more generally. It argues for a shift in the way we conceive of applying theatre and makes the case for it to be understood as a social-research method. Although this is not new, it is rarely explicitly proposed within the applied-theatre community. Theatre in this chapter is thus not a social intervention but the method of identifying possible and assessing existing interventions. Theatre is the research method itself, not the method to be researched. This chapter proposes a form of *theatre action research* for future projects, rather than investigating actual initiatives. It moves from the specific heat and dust of Ouagadougou to the general heat of the ground. It is inspired both by the quotations above and by the demands that have been placed on applied-theatre practitioners.

It is a response to those people that sit in the back of vehicles, on the backs of donkeys, and claim to understand the heat of the floor. It is a response to the pen holders who privately record the lives of others, and have the power to remake their own world by writing. It is a response to those who say that you must sit above the ground to know its warmth. It is a response to those who say that research is separate from action. It is a response to those that claim theatre should be separated from the difficult task of making the road.

Understanding and meaning arise from the struggle that takes place in interactions on the ground, not only in the pale scratchings offered by those that sit up and describe. Of course, I do not deny the irony of one 'pen holder' criticising the practice of others, but my target is the objectifying writing that emanates from backs of vehicles, which is not based on reflection derived from feeling the 'heat of the ground'. This chapter, therefore, is a response to the countless people who have asked if a particular theatre project *works*. It aims to proudly turn that frustrating demand on its head, rather than meekly stutter our reply. This chapter claims that rather than researching the object of theatre, we should counter that theatre itself is the research process. It is a means for understanding, analysing, interpreting and proposing, done by people who occupy the ground. *Theatre* is an *action* that is *research*. Theatre 'invites: it belongs to all and is costless, familiar, fun and easy to alter' and is the process of people exploring, debating, searching and changing their own lives. It is where people's own stories can be presented, heard and transformed. The problem of efficacy or 'working' should not be separate but an evolving part of this process where the people themselves are asking and debating questions. Theatre is an open means for the discovery of the impact of a full range of social processes and conditions. The act of participatory theatre can ask a community what is working. Theatre here becomes the enquiry, not the object of the enquiry. This does not deny that we should ask whether the enquiry is effective or whether the research was well conducted. We still critically examine and reflect on that process, but the theatre programme is directed towards generating an understanding of a range of different experiences. The need for a donkey rider immediately destroys the democracy that is inspired by this activity because someone is placed outside it. If we aim to challenge the automatic divisions between participant and observer, actor and audience, researcher and researched, subject and object, expert and local, insider and outsider, we cannot retrigger or recreate this split in a demand for proof. Having worked hard to feel the heat, it is destructive if some are then asked to rapidly clamber back onto the donkeys to survey the lives below.

148

Action research

It is not the purpose of this chapter to offer an extensive overview of action research; that has been expertly done elsewhere (see, for example, Anusur Rahman, 1993; Greenwood and Levin, 1998; McNiff, 1988; Zuber-Skerritt, 1996). It is the contention of this chapter, however, that many of the practices and definitions relating to action research connect very strongly to the practice of applied theatre. I am specifically referring here to participatory workshop-based theatre processes with communities, where the community members are the creators of the theatrical material. These similarities are thus the starting point for any proposal that claims that theatre can be a research method itself. To support this argument it is necessary to examine several definitions of action research, around which the chapter will be focused. Greenwood and Levin, while still maintaining a division between professional action researchers and the groups with which they are working, emphasise that this form of research is a participatory process that should lead to a more 'satisfying situation for the stakeholders' (Greenwood and Levin, 1998, p. 4). It is primarily change-focused. They continue by outlining this process in stages:

> Together, the professional researcher and the stakeholders define the problems to be examined, cogenerate relevant knowledge about them, learn and execute social research techniques, take actions, and interpret the results of actions based on what they have learnt. AR rests on the belief and experience that all people – professional action researchers included – accumulate, organise, and use complex knowledge constantly in everyday life. This belief is visible in any AR project because the first step professional action researchers and members of a community or organisation take is to define a problem that they seek to resolve. They begin by pooling their knowledge. AR democratizes the relationship between professional researcher and the local interested parties. (Greenwood and Levin, 1998, p. 4)

The process does not start at the definition of the problem, but with the pooling of knowledge – not only the everyday life issues of the group or community, but the research techniques offered by the researcher. From this moment, problems can be defined and explored, actions taken and the results reflected upon. It is important to emphasise that the process is participatory and respectful of the complex learning that is used in the everyday life of the group. The project 'cogenerates' knowledge through the research process rather than imposing it on the community or leaving it to be assumed by the researchers. The process also involves learning the 'social research techniques' in order to both know which actions are to be taken and also to reflect upon them. Action and research, words that would usually be separated as two distinct moments, are brought together within the same social process. This chapter will claim that all these elements can, and often are, incorporated into the structure of a workshop, rehearsal or devised theatre project. However, by making a shift in emphasis, these elements could be deliberately and more explicitly incorporated so that theatre *is* the process of research into particular community-identified issues, concerns or programmes.

The final point to make about the above definition is the need for an interpretation of the results of actions. Whereas this can be viewed as the final moment in a reflective cycle, more usefully it should be seen as part of an action research spiral (see Lewin, 1946). Here reflection, rather than completing a project, leads to further actions that are again reflected upon. The process does not have a clear ending. The spiral continues and necessarily multiplies. Some action research processes are large scale and lead to smaller 'spin-offs'. Others start small and can develop into a range of larger programmes. Theatre action research (TAR) must also see itself as part of a spiral, not a neatly completing circle. If a theatre workshop is examining solutions to particular problems, it must also reflect on past interventions and ask new questions. Although solutions may be offered, a single answer is never found: nor is it sought. In the same way that much postmodernism doubts the existence of an 'original', we should also doubt the final. There are pauses, satisfactory interventions and shifts in focus, but no neat victory that a researcher can claim while moving on to their next project.

Although I am making a link here between the overall structure of an action research project and a theatrical process, the connection must be taken further by examining the activity that is at the heart of

150

the action research process. According to Kemmis and McTaggart action research is:

> *Collective* self-reflective enquiry undertaken by participants in social situations [...] it is *collaborative*, though it is important to realise that the action research of the group is achieved through the *critically examined action* of individual group members. (Kemmis and McTaggart, 1988, pp. 5–6; italics in original)·

One of the questions that applied theatre often asks of the areas in which it works is how certain procedures explained in texts are performed in practice. This has been done in relating theatre practice to offending-behaviour group work. When writers spoke of getting groups of prisoners or probation clients to examine their behaviour (see Priesley and McGuire, 1985), applied-theatre practitioners asked *how* they proposed to do it. The quotation above again prompts a similar question. What is 'critically examined action' and how do you do it in practice? *Critically* implies that you are reflecting and commenting, and not accepting actions at face value. *Examined* implies that the phenomena is looked at or observed. *Action* implies that what is *critically examined* is not letters on paper, or even spoken words, but the moving, acting participant. It could be argued therefore that critically examined action should have a moving 'live' activity at its centre. However, if a group were focused on action, the assumption is that they would rarely have that action happening during the meeting. If they were concerned with cultivation methods, they could return to the field to watch people farming, but the field may be at some distance from the meeting place. If they were concerned with male violence, they would be unlikely to see it during the workshop. If they were examining discrimination in the workplace, it is unlikely they would have the prejudiced employer at their session. Critically examining action perhaps therefore requires the representation of actions during the meeting. Although clearly that may be done with written reports or spoken testimony, that representation could also be the process of creating theatre. If the actions are recreated in three dimensions, the other participants are then the audience – the examiners. My argument is that *critically examined action* happens when actions are taken from one time and space and recreated at

151

another to be investigated by the participant researchers or group members. If a participant used words to explain what these actions involved, they would miss much of the richness of that action. Speech and writing are only two possible forms of presentation. Theatrical activity, in many different forms, creates a dynamic embodied practice for analysis.

TAR is thus the use of the body *and* speech to demonstrate and explain – to 'critically examine'. It does not create moments that are more real than reported speech, and neither does it create performances that have a purely representational relationship with the 'original'. Actions are as much a form of constructed 'discourse' as is speech, but they do create a richer and more layered event from which research questions, modifications and solutions can be debated. The recreated action inevitably exists as a new activity that reworks and provides a particular commentary on that which it seeks to represent. This version is then a real moment in itself, available as a resource for the group's enquiry. On the ground communities can use theatre to explore their issues in an open forum that does not automatically impose systems of meaning. By creating images or scenes amongst themselves they have the power to check, alter, rearrange and validate the knowledge that is contained within their group. They have the power to *critically examine*. The very shifting and changing nature of a theatre process means that the research will constantly move between the realities of the participants and not be dictated by the needs of the donkey riders.

Theatre here is not an intervention to change the group or the situation that faces a particular community. Therefore, it is not an activity that in and of itself demands to be evaluated for impact. Theatre in TAR is the method used by communities to examine and propose the interventions or changes that are needed in their lives. Theatre here discovers the desired interventions and is not being framed as the actual intervention (of course the degree to which this division is sustainable can be questioned, and will be discussed later). Perhaps the community might conclude through the TAR process that there is a need for cultural work with their young people. A theatre project might become part of this. However, this would be theatre as intervention, not theatre as action research. This is not to say that the

152

methods should not be reflected upon and constantly monitored, but in TAR they are participatory research tools first.

In a development setting, TAR might be pre-project and perhaps post-project work. It is the process of a community generating the skills to explore their concerns and develop strategies for overcoming their problems. Theatre is the method through which this process takes place. This chapter takes this as the starting point to discuss a way of using TAR. It offers a broad-stroke description of how a community can use theatre as the method to research and propose interventions to improve or transform their lives. It does not claim to be inventing anything totally new, rather it aims to promote a particular focus for programmes that come under the heading of applied theatre, theatre and development or theatre and social change. It also tries to elaborate how many of the concerns expressed at a theoretical level in the book can be realised in practical theatre exercises 'on the ground'. How can theatre as a research process move communities beyond bewilderment? What is the relation between different cultural forms in this process? Clearly much of the inspiration for what I am outlining here comes from the work of Boal (Boal, 1974, 1992, 1995, 1998, 2001). My point is that the techniques of Boal although often portrayed as a means of intervening in community and group development, should be seen as an invaluable tool for participatory research; for communities to set the agenda for what interventions are in fact necessary. The shift needs to reposition them from tools for social change to a practical research methodology. My advocacy of a Boalian approach does not seek to deny the relevance of other forms or locally inspired cultural practices to a theatre action research process.

Finding the ground

For people to take the ground they must have the skills and confidence to do so. This is not automatic and importantly the ground does not welcome all and is not open to different groups in a community

153

equally. However, using the ground is premised on the fact that all can enter and all can leave – and it can be occupied by small or large groups. In addition, it is not necessarily found in one place or in one position. The ground for a workshop can be created in front of a small group of children, it can be delineated in front of the chairs of a group of women (see Campbell et al., 1999, p. 38), it can be in the community square or the privacy of a family house. It can be a classroom, church hall, sports ground or prison yard. Ground is created by walking in and on it. It is not to be created by 'outsiders' for the 'insiders'. The decision for where the ground is situated is as important for a community as the freedom to speak in it. Grounds can be small and private, large and public, under cover or in the open air. The first ground that is found might not be the best for the research process in which a community wants to engage.

In that agreed space, in order to use the tools of TAR, the group must become familiar with theatrical processes and techniques. This requires them to develop a comfort in using their own bodies in front of people but also to use their bodies to express different or unfamiliar action. If as outlined in chapter one, our bodies are made up of various layers of received actions and conventions learned and consumed from our families, friends, communities and histories; we must become aware of the constructed nature of our bodies. We must learn to improvise and create with those gestures and action marks. In addition, we must also become adept at seeing and portraying the constructions of others. These are the first stages of TAR; developing the ability to play with the 'matter of action'.

Learning ourselves

In a process that is both a learning of the research techniques and also a 'pooling of knowledge', each group must start by finding fragments of their own actions of which they can remember the root or history. Do they wave their finger like their mother, shout at their children like their father, laugh like an uncle, or swear like a friend? Do they stand like other farmers, students, teachers, teenagers, prisoners or patients? Does their walk echo that of other community members? Playing with

154

a whole range of the minute and large gestures used by group members can start to discover which belong to the realities of one's current life and which are reproductions taken from elsewhere. They might be performed differently in the now, but clearly there is a shadow of a history in an action. The way someone scratches his or her face could rework the face stroking of a grandparent. A wink could be a replay of the affection of a long-term friend. The opening moments of TAR therefore explore the way individuals use their bodies. This bare vocabulary of our action is investigated to uncover where it is an accented version of learnt moves and where the marks of previous actions become visible. This first stage develops an awareness of our own bodies and a confidence to use them in performance.

Growing familiarity with the construction of our own action should gradually shift to examining how we have improvised on the structure. Where have we changed the varying performances of our families and communities? Where have we developed new shape to older actions? Where do we improvise? When do we not improvise? When is our dance identical to that of our grandmothers, and when does a movement 'rejig' the steps of the past? The work on the fragments of ourselves is not an exercise in constructing the fixed materials that have built our characters, but the examination of how we have constructed the individual action routines that make up our life from the different parts of our history. The pooling of these fragments ensures that identification of problems is built on a shared analysis of individual and group and a common method of presentation. All performances are constructed from small and large phrases – from frowns that echo elders to major interactions learned by rote from peers. The purpose of these first exercises is to become aware of the boundaries in our lives between creative reworking, simple repetition, and action where the learnt structure is invisible. It is to understand the physical language of our bodies. How what appears natural to us is constructed. How what for us is fluent, is understood by others as heavily accented.

It is also to discover the changes created by shifting to different environments. How do we improvise with our action resources in these different spaces? How do the webs of interactions created at certain moments break down and reform in different times or places? What experiences do we have of standing bewildered, and when do we feel fully 'fitted in' to a community or situation? It is not the purpose of these exercises simply to reduce participants' understanding of themselves to a series of roles. Each real-time interaction should be unpicked to examine the origins of the marks or flourishes. Does someone's fathering owe more to their own mother or father? Role play is not the exhibition of a fixed role but the creation of a pattern of action in a given situation from the raw 'bits of behaviour' (Schechner, 2002, p. 23) intermeshing with the actions of others. If the group are only taught to recognise roles the research process will offer stereotyped performances of imagined types. By starting from the smaller action matter, we can build a more complex, shaded and creative understanding of the way we perform in everyday life. This will provide a sharper tool to analyse the complex way that a problem is played through the life of a community. Proposals for change are more likely to be developed if a group can improvise on the raw materials of action rather than the fixed lines of pre-scripted characters. This process starts an exploration of an individual's performance in order to move to the next stage, where the structures of an individual's action is linked to the conventions of a particular group or community.

Community action

The next stage moves through a series of steps. First, you must develop an awareness of how your action is seen by its audience. This might start with a vision of how your shrug, smile, swagger or strut appears to your fellow group members. In seeing their representation of aspects of your actions and you performing aspects of theirs, you also practice speaking and constructing with components of action matter. You are practising using these tools of research. Acting and performing are the deliberate construction of action from gestural, vocal and physical chunks taken from your own and others' experience. It is the creative reworking of fragments of action. By developing an awareness of the construction of your own actions, you become more able to present reconstructions of others. You are more able to replay actions that happened in the past and play possible future reactions. The most important part of this stage is to find the lines of the general and the lines of the specific. Each group will have these drawn differently. This asks where can action be compared across a community and where is it the performance of one person or group of people. The swagger of a man is constructed differently from that of a woman, the stroll of the young tilts differently to that of the old, the walk of a Brazilian might have a different shape to that of a Burkinabé. These divisions are multiplied between groups, communities and countries. This step should acknowledge and explore where the group embodies the same action components, where it has different patterns of 'behaviour' and where there are very strong differences in performance. This will again ensure that the process examines the way an issue is constructed within the particular experience of the community and how different members of that community understand or perceive it.

Divergent experiences will ensure that a simple walking pattern is performed differently both by alternative groups and within groups according to the requirements of distinct situations. The next step should be to examine not just the intergroup variations but the intersituational modifications. A walk in public is different from a walk in solitude. A walk in the home might be unrecognisable from that walk in a school or workplace. In the first stage the exploration of difference and similarity would be focused around simple single actions – handshakes, walks, runs, facial expressions, dance moves, signs of affection, displeasure and so on. The second stage would ask how a handshake (if it exists in the culture) is performed and interpreted differently according to the conventions of the moment. Is it affection or formality? When and how might it become affection rather than formality? Is it a signal of power or subservience? What conditions need to be in place for it to be understood as power rather than subservience? Learning the contours of one's action is also about learning that it is raw material that constantly shifts and only gains meaning in its execution. This part of TAR is moving from teaching people the method to exploring how it can be used.

Gradually the work will start to turn from the examination of simple sequences of actions into the exploration of miniature rituals. The group will be discussing how they as a community create interactions with their 'bits of behaviour'. They will explore the sets of activities that make up their daily routines – both the ordinary and the extraordinary. Each of these routines will be compared between people and between the variety of situations in which they occur. The work will investigate how much each person, family or community has developed new routines and how much they have borrowed or continued to use those from the past. It will also ask, if the act arose from the past, how much they have now changed it. The group will explore where there are spaces for improvisation and change inside the practices that make up our daily lives (see Roach, 1996 for a similar analysis of tradition versus improvisation in relation to carnival). Clearly certain groups and communities will have kept procedures and rituals very tightly protected and others might have chosen or have been forced to alter them radically. Some might shift happily to new ways and others might resist. The exploration of the tensions between improvisations and strict repetition must become central to developing a group's ability to use theatre to research their own lives. It is in these moments that opportunities for change might be found and it is in these divisions that many of the applied-theatre projects described in this book have flourished. Traditional practices can be a source of sustenance at moments of bewilderment (displacement, war, violence and imprisonment) but similarly they can maintain systems of exclusion, hierarchy and power (by, for example, prohibiting participation by certain groups such as women).

Tea making is an important activity performed differently between and within many cultures and communities. However, no-one makes tea in an act of spontaneous originality. We have all learned elements of the routine from a range of sources and come to execute our own improvisations on the theme. By this stage of a TAR project the group will have familiarised itself with elements of its own 'behaviour', and related it to actions of the other people in the group or community. The first stage will already have examined how individually you have improvised on the learnt performance of, to use my example, tea making. The next stage is to examine in practice

158

where these performances have similarities and where they differ. This is not only an exploration of different family and community traditions, but an inquiry into how and why different people have been able to improvise on those 'little dramatic performances' (Sheldon, 1995, p. 86). It is the physical exploration of the shift that Ortun Zuber-Skerritt notes when she claims that 'the overarching "meta-narratives" of the modern period have given way to the "little stories" of the postmodern condition' (Zuber-Skerritt, 1996, p. 169). What makes one group in the UK comfortably shift from china cups to mugs but another family feel affronted if the pot is not warmed?

Although this seems a somewhat trivial example, it does illustrate that we are all, even in the least significant moments, engaged in a process of repetition and improvisation. In creating and investigating the 'little stories' of each other, the group develops an awareness of the structure of its own actions and starts to explore the tensions and the possibilities for change within the actions of everyday life. Rather than see tea making as an activity that is just 'done', TAR turns it into a ritual to be explored.

In TAR a community is using theatre to first discover its research questions, then to gather 'data' to support an exploration of those questions and thirdly to develop proposals for change. TAR finally returns to discuss and debate the success of those interventions. At the point of developing an understanding of the construction of a community's action, we are working just before the point of discovering the important questions. Groups will have developed an awareness of common areas of performance and where there are differences. They will have found moments where certain gestures, larger rituals and practised routines echo with a common action structure that is familiar to all. They will have found other moments that divide the group along gender, age, class or other lines. The acknowledgement of these differences might be a point of acceptance and learning that is valuable in itself. However, it might be the stimulus for the separation of the group so that particular issues can be explored. It might mean that it is worth shifting the ground of the activity so that a specific group can feel they are able to participate fully. If you are working in a prison this might be difficult, in a village it might be easier. If you are working with a group of people who have

159

come together specifically because they have a connection or a common concern that they want to research, then this is less likely to happen. A group of young people with physical disabilities might find easy connections, but a disparate group of adolescents might struggle. A group that has few action fragments in common is as likely to have problems between each other as have problems that unify them. However, the experience of the first stages of TAR should find elements of routine that link even the most diverse communities. This is not to say that all groups will find some universal point of connection, rather the specifics of some groups' routines will find points of recognition in the specifics of another.

With all groups the moment of examining where individual actions find links with others can reveal possible points of connection between disconnected individuals as well as points of divergence between apparently connected ones. This stage is vital to work out whether the intervention needed is on the division itself or whether despite differences there are similarities enough for common issues to be explored. From this moment, with a group that has developed a level of competency in performing and exploring their lives, the next stage of TAR can be approached.

Analysing 'life'

TAR is about *critically examined action*. Whereas the first few stages will have already touched on many areas of community action and explored the line between improvisation and exact repetition of the matter that makes up these moments, the next stage takes this on as its central objective. A group or community are using theatre as the participatory research method to analyse their problems and concerns and where and what interventions might be relevant. One proviso to be added here is that facilitators, where they come from outside the community, must not impose problems where a community does not accept it has any. A community at peace with itself does not automatically benefit from the unearthing of unacknowledged tensions. Problem exploration can rapidly become problem creation. Of course, it may be in different people's interests to maintain that

160

there are no problems and one group's peace may be another's oppression, but still care must be taken. These boundaries can be examined, but all work must be done honestly, respectfully and with sensitivity. The ground must be a place for serious reflection but also for uninhibited celebration if the community chooses it.

The direction of this next section of a TAR project is heavily dependent on the type of group and the reason they have been brought together. A group that has assembled through their common status or issue concern will move forward differently to a group determined for example by geographical location. The central part of this next stage is to hear the stories. In the terms of Greenwood and Levin's definition of action research, here the group are identifying the problem and through this 'cogenerating knowledge' about it. This is done through an examination of how the problem is played out within people's daily reality, and not as a context free issue. It is important to hear how a specific concern sits within the narratives of their lives. Theatre can place a living, breathing and moving action around the dried out text of a 'community problem'. Drug use, AIDS, teenage pregnancy, land use and family violence do not have context-free meanings or solutions. In this analytic phase, it is not the stories that are fleshed on the bones of an issue brought to a community: it is the opportunity for a group to tell stories so that they can identify their concerns from the context of specific actions. The ideal version of this process would be that from the stories come the issues and not vice versa. However, in the world where these projects are likely to take place there will be prearranged agendas that are determined by different government and non-government agencies. This is recognised, but still the process should insist that those issues are made concrete through the embodied action of participants. Because the group will be using fragments of action which are understood to be historically and socially constructed and also specific to the demands of each situation, the issues should become embedded in the minute detail of people's lives.

With the practice in using their bodies to demonstrate and critically examine action, it is anticipated that the group will be comfortable in presenting increasingly elaborate stories. These might have been developed in a multitude of forms including still images, scenes, dances or mimes. However, this process must move from a sketch to the 'full account'. The first version of the story or stories will be like rough notes making broad points about the narrative under investigation. These must be honed gradually so that the story is worked on and agreed upon by all those in a particular group. This is not so that it is 'true' but so that it creates a version that the group wish to express. The process generates the knowledge that the group have about this particular issue. This might mean that there are different shades of the same story. Smaller groups might be finding different incidents across time or in different spaces in the community where the same rough account performs in different ways. Multiple stories might have similar issues embedded in them. The sketch becomes the 'full account' when the group agrees that the scene or scenes adequately demonstrate the problem, illustrate the knowledge they have of it and express the way that it affects their lives. The 'full account' is of course still a partial one, but it is as full a version of the account as the group wish to express or are able to construct.

The above process could be translated into short scenes showing different ways that husbands have abused their wives. It could be a movement piece portraying the arrival of a particular group to a specific locale. It could relate the moments that led to imprisonment, or common examples of mistreatment by employers. Analysing life should be as rich as the lives of those present; it should not assume what is important and what is trivial. The process should not create a hierarchy between performances of the micro and those of the macro. Huge historical injustice can be played out through minute relationships, and structural oppression can be displayed through 'mere' glances. Sibling rivalry could be as important for one group as national disputes are for another. Personal loss through suicide might be what devastates one community, whereas genocidal oppression could be the legitimate concern of another.

Playing with the 'full account'

It is not enough just to work to create the 'full account' of a particular story: that creation must also be explored through a range of performance forms. This might mean the conscious use of local cultural practices in the presentation of the story. It might be the inclusion of music, dance, puppetry or masks (see Boal, 1992, p. 243 for description of 'rehearsal of style' as a Forum rehearsal method). It might be the deliberate relocation of the naturalism of the story to new places or times. This process will further demonstrate the methods and means by which our lives are constructed from raw action material but also how we have the power to use that material in the positive recreation of new actions and narratives. In the exploration of this dimension to the group members' theatre, they are proving their ability or their potential to transform their lives. This stage of TAR has moved beyond learning the techniques, beyond using the tools to the creative use of the method. This is an aesthetic dimension that is a vital 'functional' part of the process of researching community problems. The aesthetic within the research method ensures that the investigation includes the non-linear, unpredictable, unsayable and visual as vital parts of the construction of the group's knowledge of the particular issue. It is a way of them interpreting the 'complex information' they have displayed and generated about their lives.

If the group were researching the problems in relationships between the young and the old, focused perhaps on the moment of disciplining a child, the 'analysing life' stage of TAR would have at first seen a short role play of a particular incident. Next it would examine and rework that role play in detail and the group would show examples of this action in different families, in different circumstances and across time. The playing with the 'full account' section would include the incorporation of heightened performance techniques to create visions of the disciplining action through other cultural forms. This might be as simple as the introduction of a non-familiar setting (how does the disciplining of your son change if you are the queen?) or elaborate as the use of a highly stylised dance form. This presentation gives a group both new ways of seeing that action and new ways of doing that action. From this, a richer, more complex and multiply layered interrogation of the story is more likely to take place.

Reflecting on life

From this point onwards, a group is starting to focus and systematise. In any process, they will need to make decisions about what they want to research within their group or community. This might have become obvious during the first stages or it might take a deliberate decision. Again, this is not the artificial placement of 'the issue' onto the community but a negotiation about a focus from the stories already heard. If it is agreed, for example, that family violence is the concern to be explored, the presentation of short acted stories will have demonstrated what it looks like and what it means to that particular community. For the process to continue general points of comparison must be drawn from these specifics. At this stage, the colour of actual stories needs to be maintained while asking whether there is a general archetype. A research process needs to have a question to ask about how, to keep the example, family violence affects a particular community, while still being richly supported by specific detail. The first stages of TAR have thus found the stories and started to tease the exact questions for the research project. This next stage agrees upon the main question and starts the process of exploring the boundaries of the problem and possible responses.

It depends on the type of group as to whether the process of working on and between the specific and general also becomes a wider research moment with participation from larger sections of a community. If the group were exploring the level of mine awareness in their village, or the understanding of HIV/AIDS transmission issues in their prison, presentation of the range of small stories to the wider community might be appropriate at this stage. This could happen in large groups or again amongst smaller subsections of the community. The audiences would be invited to respond, question and intervene in the pieces presented. This would not be to solve the problem that is displayed but to express their own connection or lack of connection to

164

the stories. It is important to emphasise that these small performances would not be about giving information. This is not possible if you do not know what information is needed. It would be about broadening the research community and checking the 'data' already arrived at with a wider audience.

This stage is of course not always possible or relevant. However, it is important to remember who the group is before it is accepted that its issue stories can be universally assumed to be the concerns of a larger community. A group of inmates in a prison education department might not have the same level of knowledge, issues or stories as those that do not attend education. A group of women participants might be significantly younger than the women in the wider village community. This is of course not a problem if they are only seeking to research issues that are relevant to themselves as a group. If this is the case they can check the relevance of the narratives between themselves, and articulate the questions that arise from these moments.

The whole of the TAR process has been one of asking a series of questions with a group. This has led to a 'pooling' and exhibition of knowledge. The first stage asked what are the action components of the group members' lives. The second asked how this is constructed to form the routines, rituals and 'little stories' of the everyday. The third asked how these make up larger stories of the life of group members. The fourth questioned the concerns, specific and general, that were embedded in these stories. The next checked whether these concerns were the most relevant to explore and if they touched the lives of others in the community. Only after all these stages will TAR examine what the community wants to do with the problem. It is in this final stage that the group are asked what interventions they would like to see in order to create a more 'satisfying situation' (Greenwood and Levin, 1998, p. 4).

165

In its archetypal form Forum theatre (Boal, 1992) involves short 'anti-model' scenes being presented by a section of the community to other members of the community. This is the raw research data the group have worked on. The anti-model should demonstrate the pattern the problem draws in the life of the community but it does not propose actions to be taken to resolve it. Audience members are then invited onto the stage, onto the ground, to replace the protagonist in order to take actions that will change or at least impact positively upon the problem. Maybe the protagonist is being mistreated by a fellow worker, maybe they are under threat from a husband, maybe they are a disciplined child. The audience is being asked to rehearse under the scrutiny of its peers solutions that the group members may be able to use in their lives. It is only a small shift to say that this is a research – a TAR – process. It is a public event enacted to generate knowledge that could form the basis of changes to a particular situation. Each intervention is thoroughly examined, its implications acted through and its weaknesses explored. The procedure should avoid simplistic answers, always testing and doubting interventions through the development of the narrative implications. Interventions that move from the interpersonal to the communal must be encouraged. The action suggestions must be developed beyond the scene presented to show wider implications and areas for possible change.

Forum presentations of this nature might take place within the small group, with mini-scenes being shown amongst the members and solutions proposed for each other. They also might consist of the group presenting stories and scenes to the wider community. In TAR this is the point in a research 'spiral' where proposals for action are generated that must be critically examined and presented to others where appropriate. Rehearsals of change are not assumed to lead to change. As I have noted repeatedly in this book, rehearsal is no guarantor of action. Each intervention, if accepted as appropriate by the group or community, must be analysed to see what needs to be in place to make it translate beyond the event. That analysis is done theatrically in the here and now of the larger Forum presentation or later in the smaller group workshops. If a solution proposed was after-school care for young people, the next stage would be to create a plan for that action to be realised. If an intervention demonstrated that a person's confidence helped them overcome the problem, a proposal for how a group's confidence could be increased so that all members could manage the problem would need to be developed. Each intervention must be followed by a plan for implementation.

The group might have seen an intervention displayed which they felt improved the circumstances. This now becomes their new raw material. It is the end scene of a story they must now create. What are the scenes, the narrative twists and turns that need to happen to make that final scene come about? How can those intermediate scenes be prepared for in reality? This is a form of theatre action planning that goes beyond writing a list of tasks to ask what those tasks look like in action. For example, if the intervention agreed upon was the need to get a new building constructed, this would be the final scene in a complex story that TAR allows a group to imagine before the project is started. TAR also allows that imaginary narrative to shift around the problems and obstacles that the group think might be thrown in their way. Although the final action is preordained, the group is asked to imagine the many possible points of departure and the multiple routes to this destination. This process produces its own smaller sets of problems that might be presented back to the wider community for investigation.

At some point in TAR, the fictional action on the ground of theatre must shift to action in the 'real' world. This will involve the implementation of the first proposals in the theatre action plans that have evolved from the interventions. As I have already argued, 'fictional action' cannot be repeatedly rehearsed until its future execution becomes guaranteed. The 'action plan' should be an agreed set of ideas, whose validity is still to be tested. The process makes no assumptions about the literal translation into moments of change. In addition, the fact that first ideas are now to be enacted does not mean that the TAR process is over. The group can continue to act as a sounding board for the process of change. Each stage of the planned management of the solution can be brought back to the group to be discussed and examined. Of course, to examine action, as before, you must use action. The attempt at a particular intervention, or step towards making it possible, now become the 'little story' that the group explore. These incidents become the material for the continuation of the TAR process.

Intervention or research?

This chapter has claimed that participatory theatre can become a serious research method that allows a community to analyse, present and actively set their own agenda for change. Ideally it allows people to research issues affecting their community from a basis of equality and jointly develop recommendations for action. For the purpose of the argument, I have tried to make a division between the intervention and a research process. This separation insists that a community must have the power to tell their own stories and have their knowledge of the specifics of their lives respected before interventions can be enacted. It relies on the group using their own actions and words in a process of self-examination. This model claims that intervention is only viable if it is based on a community's analysis of needs and that theatre itself in TAR is not an intervention. However, as I have also hinted, the division cannot be sustained absolutely. I have articulated the split in order to highlight a potentially fruitful way of seeing participatory theatre, not because I am seeking a new dichotomy in practice.

In fact, in is very hard to divide a pure research process from an intervention. Any activity, while claiming to be research, must be examined for how it also simultaneously affects or intervenes in people's lives. The origins of Action Research point to an emphasis that action and research should happen in parallel or simultaneously. The words were brought together to show that there should be no automatic division between researching and doing. Running a theatre session with a group therefore will be an action that affects their lives. This has been a central theme of this book. It has been argued that in the minutiae of how participants move and watch others move, they will have reflected on their own bodies. The use of any muscle, however slight, changes that muscle. This includes the 'muscles' of the brain. Systematic use of certain movements by (for example) body builders, directly marks their bodies with new forms of muscle shape and curve. However small, any physical/mental engagement in a theatre process will have developed phrases and traces that will be interventions in the embodied lives of participants. Boal's games specifically aim to refigure the body so that the people become aware of how their bodies are socialised; how they have become atrophied and hypertrophied by the world in which they act (Boal, 1992, p. 61).

In undertaking an activity that uses physical, cognitive and emotional skills, ties will have been formed between the group that were not there in the first place. The simple action of smiling with somebody connects you in a shared 'real' emotional experience. It is an intervention in your emotional repertoire that should not be dismissed or trivialised. Even if this were done in a fictionalised role play, the acts of smiling, catching someone's eye or laughing with others create affective traces and memories that must be acknowledged. Dealing with major areas of stress, trauma, community joy or loss will therefore have an even greater 'impact'. Being actively involved in a group process and especially one that requires you to physically play with incidents, stories and emotions, might be empowering in itself. It might in fact intervene to increase the power of a certain group in a community in a direct way. This is explicitly recognised by Goyder, Davies and Williamson (1998) when they state that:

> There is therefore a need for clarity on whether a participatory exercise is meant to be 'empowering' in itself, or whether it is seen as a 'means' to help an agency or group reach conclusions either about its future activities or the 'impact' of past interventions. (Goyder, Davies, and Williamson, 1998, p. 6)

Clearly, in TAR the initial impulse for the activity is the latter. The exercises are geared towards discovering what interventions might be necessary in the future. However, we must be aware that the activity itself does have effect. As I state in chapter two the 'futuritive' cannot deny the performative. In insisting that the ground is a space for democratic debate, new interactions will have occurred which might inscribe unfamiliar patterns of understanding amongst the group members. The process will not leave the participants untouched. In opening the ground to the whole TAR process, certain traditions or protocols of who is allowed to speak, when and under what circumstances, might have been undermined directly (see Campbell et al., 1999 for a direct discussion of this). For example, in giving space to a womens' group, their position might be altered in their own eyes or in the eyes of the community. The act of telling or listening to a story is not only research into problems that are revealed but an affirmation that the story is important. Telling and witnessing that telling is transformative in the moment, as well as providing inspiration or research information for the future.

The TAR process therefore has the potential to be both a community-driven research exercise and an intervention in people's lives. For this reason there are ethical questions that need to be addressed before a TAR process is started. For example, we must question who has the right to decide that this approach should happen with a particular group. If one fundamental of TAR is that the community makes the decisions about what interventions are appropriate – and discovers these through theatre – how could a community decide that it wants this intervention called theatre in the first place? How can we offer a method that is also going to intervene in people's lives without getting explicit permission or invitation? How can we acknowledge the values inherent in a process that professes not to impose values? Have we then a right to intervene, especially if we claim we are only searching for interventions?

In response to these questions, I would contend that most if not all research methods do affect the communities in which they occur, whether they are participatory or whether they are externally driven: whether they start from a commitment to sharing the ground, or whether they are dictated by the donkey riders. The briefest observation, the shortest interview and least obtrusive sampling all impact, however minutely. What TAR needs to discover is how it can be explicit about the effect it might have, and how the community can opt into the possible, varied and perhaps unpredictable results that participation could create. Clearly, no group member would ever be forced to participate, but simultaneously, those using theatre techniques must not hide their purpose or the likely results of using them. You do not pretend to be 'only' doing a community play if your intention is also research.

170

Similarly, you do not claim 'research results' having only been explicit about your aim of creating a piece of community-based theatre. Advertising a 'theatre workshop' in a prison and then using the experience as a diagnostic exercise to assess behaviour, although easy to repudiate on paper, can often happen in practice. We do not 'know what is right' for a group or community and therefore any work must rely on first an invitation and then open discussion of all the implications involved in undertaking this approach to research. The very tentative and gradual nature of the section on learning the routines and shapes of an individual's action in this proposal is due to the need for a safe framework for the participants to be able to discover and learn the techniques. This relatively gentle introduction allows participants to opt out before they have personally committed too extensively.

Did the well-digging work?

I have concentrated here on the use of the TAR process to discover and test out interventions or actions to be taken by a particular community. It should also be emphasised that TAR can be used to ask questions after an intervention. As part of a continuous process of community development, TAR would question interventions suggested by its own process, but it might also include the examination of an intervention that has already happened, recently or in the distant past. How is the school being used? What are the problems with the new pharmacy? Does the disability access to the new building function for this particular group? This is the reverse process of one discussed earlier. In TAR specific life stories are used to discover which issues are relevant and what they look like in the actions of a particular group. Here the issue – or more specifically the intervention – is brought to life, with the group fleshing the action details onto its bones. The community creates the story of using the wells to ask whether the project to dig them has worked.

Conclusions – on the 'pale scratchings offered by those that sit up and describe'

This chapter has proposed a way of conceiving an applied-theatre practice. It has suggested a shift to developing theatre as a research method rather than as a method to be researched and validated. Theatre here is not the 'mirror up to nature' but a complex reworking and interpretation of social practices, histories and memories. It is a form of knowledge and way of constructing and presenting that knowledge. Although I believe this is implicit in most theatre practice, the chapter has sought to propose that this could become explicit in applied theatre's engagement with the contexts in which it works. While projects have been devised with this intent, it is rarely articulated as directly as I am expressing it here. This chapter is thus a proposal, a rehearsal, for projects that do not yet exist. As a rehearsal it is of course idealised and bears a tenuous relationship to any TAR initiatives that might be developed. For these reasons, my conclusion is cautionary.

I have already acknowledged the irony in criticising 'donkey riding' when this chapter could be challenged as an exercise in just that. These are 'pale scratchings' and therefore they too are meaningless unless they become connected to a form of *critically examined action*. The gaps in this proposal, although admitted, can be filled only through the action that this chapter suggests. I cannot overcome these inadequacies by disconnected brain toil at a computer. I need to get on the ground and start to practice TAR to discover its tensions, weaknesses and flaws. Obvious problems might be found in the length of time it takes to get a group comfortable in the use of their own bodies. Can a marginalised community really give up that much time? Another problem might be in the expectations about physical activity in a community where the movement of participants' bodies may be prohibited or severely restricted. However, these and other problems will only really be discovered through the self-reflection of the TAR process itself. I have presented an idealised version of a road that will only be made by walking. This proposal therefore needs to feel some heat.

Chapter Five
Becoming ethical

> Suddenly and without prior indication, they are in the middle of an ethical minefield. (Cohen and Manion, 1994, p. 348)

> Becoming ethical is not merely a rational endeavour – it involves imaginative shifting of positions to extend experience to include multiple and often conflicting views of events. (Edmiston, 2000, p. 64)

This final chapter seeks to question some of the ethical issues involved in a series of applied-theatre training projects that were run in Sri Lanka during 2000. This book has sought to demonstrate the complexity of the use of theatre as part of development, prison education and participatory community projects. It has also questioned the relationship between principles of practice and the specifics of application. It has taken the concept of bewilderment to indicate the shift between a necessary clarity and a creative confusion, as well as the problems of a value-based practice constantly tested by the flexibility demanded by context. These issues become the central concern of this final chapter, bringing the dazzle of bewilderment into the minefield of ethics.

The practice of applied theatre in places of armed conflict raises acute questions of ethics and responsibility. The minefield from Cohen and Manion's opening quotation is, in Sri Lanka, literal and metaphorical. In a situation where the whole notion of what it means to be a citizen is highly and violently contested, dialogue-based participatory theatre work treads a difficult and sometimes dangerous path. The ability to research, question and set agendas offered in the proposal from the previous chapter is tested by this troubled context. This chapter aims to explore these issues through the analysis of three examples or moments taken from larger theatre projects. The chapter will raise certain questions of ethics through these stories, rather than giving a detailed overview of the projects themselves. By doing this I hope to question the appropriateness of using theatre in conflict situations and set out some tentative points to contribute to the overall debate in the book. The confusions of entering prisons, the search for principles in Freire and Boal, the narrative of loss and the problems of translating theatre forms in new settings, are all touched upon by the problems discussed here.

I will frame my analysis of these 'stories' through a number of different theoretical terms. These are used to inform the writing and the practice that it discusses and are taken from Valentine Daniel's book on what he calls an 'anthropology of violence' in Sri Lanka (Daniel, 1996). In discussing the interplay and tensions between communities that experience their lives through the organising force of either history or myth, Daniel provides a valuable terminology for the way people participate or see their place in a society. He divides between an *epistemic* and an *ontic* view, whereby the former concentrates on how a group sees the world and the latter how they exist in the world. One is concerned with seeing, studying and observing and the other with being and participating. Daniel uses these terms to compare the imperial, mostly British influence on what was Ceylon, and the 'lived in' experience of myth and ritual that characterises a number of the communities in Sri Lanka. The linear chronology of European history is given a counterpoint in the circularity of Indian/Sri Lankan myth and religion. The process that created a history – an epistemology – of first arrivals, invasions and supremacy between rival Buddhist Sinhala and Hindu Tamil groups is, according to Daniel, implicated in the violence that has beset the island since 1983.

I will use these terms as a reference point to several of the problems related in this chapter. They will inform two distinct but connected parts of the debate. First, the division relates to my writing, and the actual ethical problems of constructing a text from my experience. Although interrogating this practice is vital, I believe the power to question and the ability to answer clearly is negotiated between these two concepts. I accept Jane Plastow's demand that we should 'take on board what seem [...] fundamental questions' (Plastow, 1998, p. 98), but the ability to ask what she later calls the 'unsentimental' (Plastow, 1998, p. 99) is mediated by the relationship

174

the writer has to the material. Plastow assumes that we in the West are freer to speak and thus in an epistemic relation to the work. Rather than automatically giving us a responsibility to speak out, I believe that this places us in a dubious position related and not necessarily in opposition to the oppressive epistemology project of the West criticised by Daniel. It positions us as the knower, the organiser, the categoriser – the theoriser – that sits us within an ethically suspect practice not outside it. It links us to the problems of the donkey riders, discussed in the previous chapter.

Second, these terms will be related to the actual courses that I ran and how people participated in them. The epistemic and ontic will be examined as particular strategies of participation. Although it has been noted (see Schonmann, 1996) that the danger caused by working with theatre in conflict situations is due to the fact that 'participants oscillate between reality and unreality' and that oscillation creates a 'polar encounter between a tense life situation and a fictional situation' (Schonmann, 1996, p. 185), I believe that the problem lies in oscillation between the epistemic and the ontic; between participation in theatre and a desire to know techniques. This will be explained further in discussion of the stories outlined below.

My use of the terms 'epistemic' and 'ontic' in response to the problems of writing will be linked to two additional concepts that exist as strategies to counter the dilemmas faced. I will use the terms 'explanatory' and 'evocative' to indicate writing that shifts from the project of epistemology to a more open-ended, deliberately less theorised telling. It is difficult for academic writing to move in any other direction than that of epistemology. By putting pen to paper, we engage in the generation of ways of seeing the world. We generally are encouraged to have an epistemic and thus explanatory relationship to our material. However, I believe that an evocation that elicits responses from rather than elaborates theories for the reader is at times the most appropriate writing style. Saldaña in writing about the ethics of ethnographic performance states that he 'deliberately [withheld] overt theoretical commentary to make this text evocative rather than explanatory' (Saldaña, 1998, p. 185). The desire to give primacy to the evocative seems to originate in the fear of being forced into what Cohen and Manion call a 'procrustean system of ethics' (Cohen and

Manion, 1994, p. 349). If, as I have stated above, the very epistemology that explanatory writing develops is implicated in the violent situation from which the experiences discussed arrived, a shift away from direct theorising must be attempted.

The final section of this chapter is an attempt to discover what 'evocation' could be, rather than a definitive example of it. The inspiration for this comes from the ethnography of Stephen Tyler. The place of evocation rather than explanation is aligned to his belief that 'the rhetoric of ethnography is neither scientific nor political, but it is, as the prefix ethno- implies, ethical' (Tyler, 1986, p. 122). In his elaboration of a postmodern ethnography, he goes on to explain his understanding of the 'art' of ethnography:

> It is, in a word, poetry – not in its textual form, but in its return to the original context and function of poetry, which, by means of its performative break with everyday speech, evoked memories of the *ethos* of the community and thereby provoked hearers to act ethically. (Tyler, 1986, p. 126)

My edge towards the actual 'textual form' of poetry later in this piece is thus an attempt at 'a performative break' done in order to evoke/'provoke' rather than explain.

My belief that explanation itself is ethically problematic, is linked to debates in studies of ethics between relativism and absolutism; from a position that maintains that there are no universally applicable standards to one that claims that absolute principles do exist. I have instinctively accepted a move away from a (Kantian) belief in fixed moral values that can be applied universally (see Edmiston, 2000) and tended to agree that ethical values are relative and 'each research undertaking is an event *sui generis*' (Cohen and Manion, 1994, p. 349). This instinct however is questioned by the experiences related here, and has been troubled by many of the different examples offered in the book. Relativism is hard to maintain when the explanatory or epistemic project of writing on ethical dilemmas moves in the direction of 'standards', even when we insist they are formed from the specificity of practice. Edmiston gives a clear but understandable version of this when at one point he appropriately explains that:

Values are not acquired from outside us, but rather, they are forged in dialogue among people and texts. Thus, encounters with stories or people, in everyday life and in the imagination of drama, are sites for dialogue through which we can become clearer about the ethical views we or others already hold and through which our ethical positions can change. (Edmiston, 2000, p. 64)

Although this formulation underpins much of the perspective developed in this chapter, by the end of his piece Edmiston talks of these changing positions being 'grounded in ethical assumptions he or she brings to each particular encounter' and that he makes 'no apology about [his] advocacy of kindness, respect' (Edmiston, 2000, p. 81). He thus has an ethical code that is formed prior to the 'encounter'. One of the central problems noted throughout this book is that within claims to ethical relativism a Kantian ghost lurks, and this haunts any explanatory account that seeks to discuss the ethics of practice. Through the experiences discussed here, I make the claim that rather than exorcising that presence, we need to acknowledge it more freely. Although 'evocation' can be a strategy to avoid the imposition of personal values, the principles I bring to this work should be a central part of the discussion, not a problem to be elided. We should not be embarrassed about the absolutes that we might inadvertently advocate. Principles have proved useful to question and develop practice, and cannot only be framed as dangerous impositions.

My final point of introduction is a more general one. The exploration of ethics of practice in applied or community theatre is not a peripheral debate. Ethical questions should not be 'denigrated or derided as one of the typically modern constraints now broken and destined for the dustbin of history' (Bauman, 1993, p. 2); rather, they need to be 'dealt with, in a novel way' (Bauman, 1993, p. 4). We should take on the challenge of Paul Rabinow's 'critical, cosmopolitan intellectual' who has trouble with the 'balancing act' between 'reifying local identities or constructing universal ones' (Rabinow, 1986, p. 258). In addition, we need to remind ourselves of the Freirian mission to avoid 'cultural invasion' where 'the actors [...] superimpose themselves on the people' and attempt 'cultural synthesis' where the 'actors become integrated with the people, who are co-authors of the action' (Freire, 1970, p. 161). 'Co-authoring' is another term that implies the need for a balancing act between the imposing moral absolutist and the relativist. This 'balancing act' has of course been the struggle through the mist of bewilderment that has characterised the core of this book. However, the 'beyond' of the title is here offered as the need to acknowledge that the balancing itself is a powerful generator – not inhibitor – within the field.

Etymologically the work of theatre is linked to seeing and theorising through its Greek root of *thea* meaning 'to see'. It is tied to the epistemic. The work of ethnography is, as explained by the quotation from Tyler, explicitly linked to *ethos* and ethics. For Rabinow's 'critical cosmopolitan intellectual' 'the ethical is the guiding value' (Rabinow, 1986, p. 258). Any ethnographic account of a theatre practice will therefore at its heart be dealing with the ethics of knowing and seeing. It is a 'balancing act', struggling on the edge of the ontic/epistemic, the evocative/explanatory and the relativist/absolutist that we must engage in. This chapter therefore represents a few nervous steps along that edge, with frequent admissions of where I have been blown from side to side.

Sri Lanka

> It involves differences in the conception of the past, in the terms used to describe reality, and in the grasp of what the future character of the state should be. (Schonmann, 1996, pp. 175–6)

> Bits broke and drifted away and we were left with this spoiled paradise of *yakkhas* – demons – and the history of mankind spoken on stone. (Gunesekera, 1994, p. 84)

Sri Lanka is a country that has been affected by nearly twenty years of civil war. Until the ceasefire of 2002 was signed, it was predominantly fought out between the forces of the Sri Lankan Army (SLA) and the Liberation Tigers of Tamil Eelam (LTTE). I do not propose to give a detailed history of the conflict here (see Gunaratna, 1998; De Silva, 1998; Narayan Swamy, 1994; Rotberg, 1999; Wilson, 2000), partly

178

because any attempt to do so would automatically adopt the narrative forms and assumptions held by one of the many differing shades of opinion on the island. As Schonmann describes in her analysis of the Israeli–Palestinian conflict the very 'terms used to describe' are contested. Immediately to lead on from my discussion above, the process of explaining or summarising would be to *join in* the dispute that has claimed more than sixty thousand lives since 1984 (Rotberg, 1999). In Sri Lanka where the 'conception of the past' is disputed, to engage in explanation cannot be conveniently separated from *participation in* the dispute that is played out as violent conflict. One of Jane Plastow's 'fundamental' questions for 'theatre for development' practitioners becomes problematic in the Sri Lankan context. She asks 'how useful, empowering or valid can Theatre for Development be if it is constantly fearful of engaging with some [...] areas of debate, in case this will be seen as meddling in politics?' (Plastow, 1998, p. 98). The problem presented in Sri Lanka is that any action, any statement or any event can be seen or read as 'meddling in politics', and therefore while the fear will still be there, you cannot avoid participation. The places I have visited, the organisations that I worked with, the individuals on the courses, were read in different ways by different people. Some of those readings interpreted my actions as 'taking sides'. They placed me as a participant, in an ontic relationship with the work and the situation in the country. The researcher's desire to know was pitted against a situation that demanded, at some times more strongly than at others, that I was part of the situation. Whether you are 'constantly fearful' or not, it is rare to have the power to control how you are seen. I suspect that the anxieties about how and where to practice that this fear creates do not have an automatic relationship to the degree to which the theatre is valid or useful.

My connection with Sri Lanka goes back to when I was a volunteer and teacher in a prison in the south in 1985. This chapter, however, seeks to discuss theatre training programmes run as part of a project funded through UNICEF and other NGOs for groups of professionals who work with young people affected or traumatised by the conflict. The people on the courses were teachers, playworkers, NGO staff, theatre activists, womens' group members, psychologists

179

and young people themselves. In 2002 there was a growing number of applied-theatre projects in Sri Lanka supported by a strong network of practitioners called Big Circle. These individuals and organisations have created and continue to develop some astonishingly powerful and innovative theatre programmes in an immensely diverse and challenging range of settings.

The discussion of the ethics of this work is to be focused around three incidents that took place during my visits to the island in 2000. This is not meant to be an attempt to explain the specifics of theatre work with war-trauma survivors, but to elaborate on moments of doubt that might evoke responses from writers and practitioners in a range of educational or applied-theatre settings. I write not as the observer, recorder or researcher of these incidents but as the person running the courses. I was co-generator with the course participants of each moment. As with all commentary in this chapter, therefore, the epistemic business of explanation cannot be detached from my participation in, my 'ontic' relation to, the work.

Story 1: the road-block scene

During my visit in January 2000 I was asked to conduct a training course with community-theatre workers and professionals who worked with young people in the northern town of Jaffna. Although no more than 250 miles from the capital Colombo, this town was completely cut off from the rest of the country, with the only access at that time by a twenty-two-hour Red Cross boat journey from the eastern port of Trincomalee. Jaffna is the heart of the Sri Lankan Tamil community and at that time was under the control of the Sri Lankan Army. During the visit the LTTE was understood to be gaining ground and shelling was heard close to the city at all times. The whole experience of working in a town with a large number of road blocks and a high presence of military on the streets brought into focus Plastow's question of 'the relationship between political

180

freedoms and the development of theatres of empowerment' (Plastow, 1998, p. 98). Whereas I would agree that the question has been 'elided by many' (Plastow, 1998, p. 98), there was no sense that the restriction of the former had automatically resulted in the dilution of the latter. Although street theatre outside the university was restricted, there was evidence of rich and varied theatre activity in Jaffna. Despite the assertion by Obeyesekere that 'the civil war in the North and East and the tensions and disruptions it caused had made Tamil theater almost non-existent' (Obeyesekere, 1999, p. 15), Jaffna demonstrated a lively theatre scene during 2000 that existed both in spite of and *because of* the situation. The Theatre Action Group, the Centre for Performing Arts and the Theatre Studies Department at Jaffna University alone, are evidence of a powerful theatre tradition that has played a major role in the cultural, social and political life of the region.

I ran four days of workshops in Jaffna on participatory theatre techniques for young people. Although welcomed by most of the participants, it must be emphasised that my input was interacting with a strong practice of youth and children's theatre that has flourished during the war period. On day three of the course, the group created a scene in which two young people were stopped at an army checkpoint. There was a checkpoint outside the hall where we worked so this was an immediate reality for the participants. In the scene, a man was let through leaving his woman companion behind. The male soldier told his woman soldier colleague to go for lunch. She left and the soldier advanced on the lone woman. At this point the scene stopped.

The group questioned the man playing the soldier. The questioning got tough, accusatory, and interrogatory. There was a sense of tension in the room, that clearly related to Schonmann's belief that danger in this type of theatre work is met in the oscillation between a 'tense live situation and a fictional situation' (Schonmann, 1996, p. 180). However, I do not believe tension itself is the problem here. The real concern is related to (paraphrasing Edmiston), the ethical assumptions I brought to this particular encounter (Edmiston, 2000, p. 81).

The first dilemma, therefore, is related to the responsibilities of the facilitator in this type of situation. When doing prison theatre I have argued that it is the facilitator's responsibility to develop the perspective-taking abilities of the group (see Thompson, 1999a, for example). The workshop should aim to push participants to a position where they can accept that more than one version of a story might be true. This moment provided me with an 'encounter with stories [...] through which we can become clearer about the ethical views we or others already hold and through which our ethical positions can change' (Edmiston, 2000, p. 64). So, while I became clear that I held a position of the need to 'relativise' the truth of a single story, I was challenged as to whether it was my duty through this dialogue to demand changes or push my preference. How could I be Freire's 'co-author', when my script would counter their clarity? Clearly in Jaffna with the army outside the room and the sound of shells falling only a few miles away, 'seeing another story' seemed harder to insist upon. Initially this 'encounter' encouraged me to give coherence and guidance to the group's perspective rather than to advocate the importance of hearing the voice of the other. The account of soldiers oppressing the local population was an important challenge to the narrative of the army of occupation. Perhaps it was right to give the group space to tell this particular story?

However, the specifics of the situation did not so easily shift the ethical position I brought. My belief that ethics are forged through practice and in dialogue was challenged by the difficulty I had in shedding my own position. My distrust in universal values became the universal value that I sought to impose, because in this particular situation I did ask the group to shift their focus. I wanted them to avoid a simplistic or stereotypical portrayal, and so we turned to ask questions of the woman soldier. I encouraged them to explore why was she there and imagine aspects of her background. They suggested amongst other things that she was from a poor village and joined the Sri Lankan army for the money. The group added some depth to the face at the checkpoint and were asked to move away from what I thought was the easy confrontation with the person playing the male soldier.

That evening I heard of a fourteen-year-old girl who had been raped by SLA soldiers. Colleagues arranged a place for her to be looked after in a convent; the only safe place in the circumstances. I was sickened by the fact that we had seen a pale ghost of that horror in the workshop. And by the fact that I had pushed them to see the character beyond the uniform of the soldier. Had I asked them to see (thea-tricalise) something that we should not see? To empathise with the occupier, the rapist? In my facilitation, I sought to complicate the single narrative, but by doing that perhaps I was also undermining the single-minded sense of direction that a community in struggle needs if it is to overcome virulent oppression. Organising against the rapist is harder in a community if you insist the story of the rapist must be heard. This tragedy did shift my position, and for the remainder of the course I allowed the dominant story the group sought to voice to pull me along. The workshop became increasingly a celebration of their unity and the narrative they were desperate to tell.

Schonmann quotes one of the students in her study of theatre projects in the Israeli-Palestinian conflict who met similar problems with seeing the other. She is reported as saying 'we are still not far from the events, we live within them [...] it is actually impossible to present or even represent the other side with true emotional involvement' (Schonmann, 1996, p. 179). This highlights another aspect of this moment that partly illustrates why my position was challenged so strongly. There is an assumption in similar training courses in the UK that participants are there to learn techniques to apply in their workplaces. Often I work with the professionals, not the young people directly. In these courses the material touched upon, although relevant to the participants, tends to be viewed from a certain distance. The participants are not the young people that are discussed, and would not see themselves (usually) as having the same problems. I would call this an epistemic relationship to the material. In Jaffna, the course was set up with this epistemic assumption. I was working with the professionals who would work with others who were affected by the war. However, within the first few exercises the futility and misguidedness of this assumption was made clear. In a war situation, and particularly in Jaffna, there was no neat distinction between those affected and the professionals who supported them. The group I worked with were directly and tragically affected by the war, and they spent their lives working with others that were similarly damaged. The desire for the comfort of the epistemic training course was thrown out with the rawness of an ontic involvement in the whole workshop process. This group were not 'far from the events' but clearly 'living in them', giving them a fundamentally different relation to the material that arose.

At the port on the day I left Jaffna, I had to wait several hours to reboard the Red Cross boat. A young Sri Lankan soldier asked me for one of the small calendars that UNICEF had been giving away. He was twenty-three and looked about eighteen. He was the youngest son of a family of four and lived in a village near Colombo. He put the calendar in his wallet that was jammed full of pictures and letters. The wallet was then put in a pouch, next to the one that had his grenade. I found myself thinking that every soldier that was killed – and many thousands have been – would have such wallets full of personal mementoes. The sweep of the workshops had propelled me to an easy place where I too started to see the army as the faceless other. I had been pulled by the ontic relationship the participants had to the stories of violence, torture and family bereavement. The face of this boy forced me to stare at where the logic of that position was taking me.

The workshop had also propelled me backwards in my theatre-practice history to a form of political theatre where single stories were celebrated. The introduction outlined how I thought I had made a 'break' from a didactic theatre in the blurred lines of a prison theatre experience. However, these projects in Jaffna, inspired by Boal and Freire, illustrated how close to the surface of applied theatre that familiar propagandist theatre of my past still lurks. Jane Plastow, in her explanation of the link between a propaganda theatre and 'Theatre for Development' (TFD), constructs a chronology between these forms connecting their development to the move between a war and a post-war situation. Perhaps I had been naive to think that a practice inspired by a participatory TFD could take root in a place where the war continued. However, the meeting with the young soldier had reminded me that the shift from the agitprop to the transitive theatre of Boal was a 'break' in methodology, not a smooth chronological inevitability. I disagree with Plastow's differentiation in the following quotation:

184

It is necessary to differentiate between propaganda theatre by oppressed groups which may contain many of the elements of, and be a precursor to, true Theatre for Development, and state sponsored propaganda theatre which is necessarily interested in the maintenance of power and the preservation of the political *status quo*. (Plastow, 1998, pp. 102–3; italics in the original)

By concentrating on the content of the theatre, she forgives the form. 'True' TFD (whatever it may be) should admit a break from this propaganda past. The argument that one practice is legitimate because it is done by the oppressed has some frightening consequences during a war situation. To put it bluntly: if torture is done in the name of the oppressed, does it make it any more acceptable than if it is done to 'maintain power'? A Kantian absolutist ghost certainly haunts my position here.

It is stating the obvious to say that any workshop facilitator in a conflict situation is not some neutral arbiter between the participants and the issues that they present. I do not simply pose problems or ask questions. The facilitator has the power to direct the focus of the inquiry for the audience. By questioning the soldiers in the road-block scene I was not simply 'not siding' with either community, nor seeking some pretend balance. I was actively seeking an end to the conflict because I saw an origin of conflict as the insistence that there was one story. Although my practice did shift with the positions that I met in this workshop, another experience, the interaction with a young soldier, edged me back to the belief that insisting on the truth of one story was a step away from silencing the other. What troubled me was that rather than a 'balancing act', I was simply falling to one side or the other with the slightest experiential push.

Story 2: the armed-men scene

After Jaffna, I went to the city of Anuradhapura further south. I ran a three-day workshop with a mixed group of Sinhalese, Tamil and Muslim participants. All were from NGOs and agencies that worked with marginalised communities and young people.

185

Out of the tense war zone of Jaffna and with a mixed group, new ethical concerns arose. Rather than pushing to hear the detail of more than one story, I found myself pulling back from telling real stories at all. The overwhelming ontic relationship with the material that arose during the workshop with the Jaffna group, was countered with a more epistemic, distanced participation by this group. My first impression was that this was because the group was more experienced than the Jaffna trainees and therefore more familiar with the position of 'learning techniques to implement with others'. However, this view was gradually undermined as I understood how much the response was again conditioned by the specifics of the Sri Lankan situation.

I will discuss one precise moment where this was realised. On the first day of the course, the participants were creating sculpted images in small groups. With only the slightest stimulus from me, the group presented an array of harrowing scenes. Three consecutive tableaux of the impact of a bomb on the life of a family; a mother desperately trying to save the lives of her children caught in cross-fire between two opposing snipers; a social-service official forcefully taking a child from a house. The lack of identification of the two snipers was of course significant, but this refusal to label was even more marked in the final group's tableaux series. The main image showed a domestic scene in which a distressed woman was crouched on the floor and two military men were restraining two 'sons', with a third apparently dead on the floor. It was the reading of this image and the subsequent translation that hinted at the difference between this group and the one in Jaffna. A Sinhala-speaking woman read the scene and then the translator gave it to me in English. 'These are the army' he started. He was immediately shouted down. The various English-speakers told him that what the woman had said was 'armed men' not 'army'. The difference was vital enough to provoke the group into this urgent act of retranslation. Here the group, instead of the rapid and specific identification of the army that happened in Jaffna, sought not to name who the perpetrators were. The diversity of the group made that impossible. The group could be unified by the idea that armed men threatened families, but were not prepared to say openly from which community these men came. 'Army' would have clearly indicated that they were from the Sri Lankan Army not the

186

LTTE. My usual questioning as a facilitator at these moments would seek detail; story – who are these armed men, why are they fighting, what are they thinking? However, the material had to be kept at a distance if the group could successfully work together. I suddenly felt that to develop an inter-community dialogue in this situation, I must *not* ask questions.

I had shifted the direction of the Jaffna workshop and only repositioned myself on meeting the young SLA soldier on my return. Here in Anuradhapura the group created for itself an unspoken ground rule, and it was when we got close to breaking that rule that most tension occurred. Trauma could be displayed, but your view of who caused it (armed men, not the army) was kept quiet. Common ground between the group could be built on an understanding of the personal impact of war and family violence. That common ground came closest to falling away when the political became public. For safety this theatre workshop replaced the concept of the 'personal is political' with the dictate that the political should remain personal or private. This rule was not articulated, but only revealed in moments when it was transgressed.

The desire the group had shown to keep the workshop unspecific and thus distanced from the named reality of their situations at first made me assume that their work would be less powerful. I had implicitly accepted Jane Plastow's critique of TFD that only deals with community issues and not the political. For her TFD needs to be free from the 'taboo':

> [It] can only be empowering if it operates freely to promote debate about every aspect of people's lives. As soon as specific areas are declared taboo this effectively disempowers the people, and [the] theatre project is then in danger of being repressive, not liberating, because people are constantly being told that in actual fact their voices, their opinions are not allowed. (Plastow, 1998, p. 98)

However, here in a workshop at which representatives from all communities in Sri Lanka were working together, a taboo was created in order to promote free debate. It was clear throughout the workshop that as soon as a scene became too close to a real situation, the tension level rose in the room and this closed and prevented the dialogue. They were all participants in the situation in Sri Lanka and therefore

187

they needed to maintain an epistemic relation to the material when working between communities. They had come to be trained how to do, and did not wish to experience or 'live in', the work. However, by maintaining their position as trainees, when actual trauma caused by the war was discussed, the debate was able to bring the group together because the specific cause of that hurt had not been named. As Schonmann states 'to improve mutual [...] understanding of the other culture, direct daily and lively contact between the two is essential' but this is done 'on the level of activity' (Schonmann, 1996, p. 176). The activity here was a training course and by concentrating on keeping it at that distance, ironically the personal connections became easier to make. Plastow asks 'without freedom to discuss any issue fully how can we talk about giving voice to the people or promoting democracy and empowerment?' (Plastow, 1998, p. 102). Although a reasonable question, the context of continuing war in Sri Lanka would have made such openness an impediment to everyone's having a voice.

I am unsure as to whether this rule would have application in other cultural work in places of conflict, but in working across communities I realised here that the act of questioning could have created dispute and further conflict. Open discussion can be built in places where personal trauma is proclaimed and respected, but that had to be pulled back from real lived experience so that emotive political finger-pointing did not replace genuine dialogue. Pointing a finger was a desire expressed through the Jaffna workshop and an action that built a unifying experience, but doing the same in Anuradhapura would have meant pointing a finger at another participant. The ethics of working in this situation meant that I had to learn when not to ask questions and to respect the silences. In a sense, maintaining an epistemic relation to the techniques presented in the course allowed a dialogue based on the ontic experience of war trauma to develop. Theorising causes or political solutions ('meddling in politics') would have disturbed or perhaps destroyed the basis for that dialogue.

Story 3: child soldiers

My final example comes from a visit to Sri Lanka in July 2000. It continues to present for me some profound questions about the context in which the work took place. My concern about the relevance of 'doing theatre' when I could hear shelling in Jaffna was dissipated by the enthusiasm and hunger that the group had shown for the work. The concern about the context of this next example remains long after the project has been completed.

During a visit to Sri Lanka in July 2000, I worked in a rehabilitation camp with child soldiers and young men who had apparently surrendered from the main anti-government armed group, the LTTE. The 'apparently' is related to the fact that there were competing stories as to where these young men were from and what actions had resulted in them being detained. As I say above, this example, rather than illustrating ethical problems arising from moments in the process, is presented because it questions the ethical basis on which we as theatre workers seek out these challenging groups in the first place.

The young men were held in a rehabilitation centre in the middle of the country in the mountainous region famous for its tea plantations. They were all Tamil in an area that has a mixed population. In the week before the project started, I found myself asking when doubts about a situation should make us refuse to undertake the work. When should questions about the 'camp' make me unwilling to do a theatre programme with a group of thirty young men? Part of this unease was a concern that here I stepped over the line of trainer or researcher to become active participant. Of course, all the workshops I have completed in Sri Lanka have taken me across that line in some way. I have never just studied the war, but have been making interventions that in some way position me as a critic of it. However, the intervention I was making here was less clearly placed in relation to that conflict. I could not dismiss my worries about participation with the soothing thought that at least I was on the side of those working for peace. If this was a government-run centre seeking to rehabilitate ex-fighters so that they could return to their communities and were no longer part of the LTTE, were we, in agreeing to undertake the project, working for that government in their mission to undermine the Tamil Tigers? Or were we really working for the 'boys' – the familiar name given by some in the Tamil community for the LTTE fighters?

'Story 3' is therefore different in that it is the whole project that concerns me. It is more recent, troubling and unfinished. Because of this, I shift writing style completely. This is a tentative attempt at the evocation discussed in the introduction, done because the act of explanation would be inappropriate. The link between explanation and justification that always exists would be too strong. This link needs to be even more determinedly worried apart in light of the postscript that appears at the end of this chapter, and was mentioned at the beginning of the book as a frame around which many of the debates have been formed. The report for this story therefore is deliberately written in a different style – more jagged, with more questions and in note form. I do not claim that this is the only way to 'evoke', but I have taken my lead from the ethnographer Tyler and worked in a style that 'is, in a word, poetry – [a] performative break with everyday speech' (Tyler, 1986, p. 126).

Bindunawewa

In a long tin shed with flapping corrugated windows.
On top of a hill.
On top of the world according to one boy.
The cracking and smacking of the glassless air holes played an un-rhythmic backing to the whole day.
The room trying to take off.

At one end the Hindu Kovil, in one corner the Buddhist shrine and at the end, around the corner a Christian altar.

Instructors (few) and trainees many, some young and some younger
The amputees were involved in the games – better at some.

190

All played with the same youthful exuberance that any group would.
Slowly they created images that by the end of the day were sharp,
crisp, rich and detailed.
Is there a responsibility to tell their stories,
Tell this story
Or tell no story?

Ethically my tattered wings were (are) flapping.
I have responsibility because I have searched out this work

Perhaps this place is where it ends.
In searching for applied theatre's heart,
of where it can logically go,
of the darkness it can possibility face,
I find boys, young men playing cricket.

The boundary fence wire is threaded with coloured creepers.
Garlands for the green corrugated halls,
Flapping their windows, trying to fly.
Seeing them safely off, or wrapping them safely in.
The young men slip of their slipoffable shoes and enter the triple holy
place.
Good morning, I have come with my friends to do some theatre.

Theatre in the places to stop the dinner party cutlery mid-mousse.
Theatre in prisons, done that darling, but with child soldiers – ooh
and aagh.

My ethics clink and clank with the forks and the knives.
Failing to fly from the top of this mountain
And thinking about staggering to the hill that is
Just Over the Next Ridge.
Child soldiers – done that – what is there for dessert?

There is a logic to this theatre work – adolescents, captives, crisis,
violence, rehabilitation.

This group presented a joyful mixture of reticence, delight, disruption and creative freedom.
In a micro micro project I deliberately steer around their trauma, finding moments of lightness; tangential stories
Opportunities for talking and reading and telling
that tug at the hems of the
Reason They Are Really There.
But never wear the full dress.
Threads snagged by games that weave around their trauma – Garlanding it.
Seeing it safely away, or wrapping it safely in?

'Ethical minefield' is a trivialising metaphor when three have lost their legs in mines.

The final image series showed the emotions of hope, fear and joy translated into stories of father–son relations, weddings, lovers' conflicts and cricket.
Of course, cricket.

In applying theatre, I creep into the discourse that I am operating within so that the project can translate, adapt and grow from the understanding of those for whom I am working.
I struggled here
I flapped and flipped between clarity and total confusion because I could not find the discursive home or homes that constructed this place.
What was happening here, for what reason?
Rehabilitation for what, to what?
Child protection?
Counter terrorism?
Vocational training?
Helping child soldiers?
Containment of surrendees?

Not knowing was fine.

But suddenly being here made us all vulnerable to the discourses
other groups chose to frame our work. In the absence of us claiming
an interpretative zone for this project, we were in danger of
succumbing to the categorisation of others.
And in a Conflict Situation that it dangerous.
Young people deserve to have programmes of work – wherever,
whenever. But...
Maybe this is the top of a mountain where we should have said 'no'.

I am used to finding uneasy compromises to make theatre work
happen. Prisons forced our hands here – but we found places of
comfort within prison regimes that could provide a theoretical home
for the practice.
In a war zone, neutrality is not a place you can easily occupy.
All territory is contested.
Even tops of mountains
Seeing me safely, wrapping me in,
Perhaps this place is where it ends.

The work with child soldiers could be claimed by the government as a
sign that they were rehabilitating the young people oppressed by the
LTTE. The LTTE could say that this project was interfering with the
war and therefore siding with the government. They were fighting for
the right to be citizens of a new nation, while we were constructing
citizens within the boundaries of a state they sought to abolish. The
Sinhalese community could (and some did) say that working with
Tamil child soldiers was another sign that applied-theatre programmes
prioritised the Tamil community over the Sinhala community. Some
groups could say we were part of a programme that trained spies,
others could say that these were collaborators, others that they were
terrorists and deserved prison, not theatre. I had to skirt around why
we were really there, because no one was prepared to say why the
young men were really there.

Conclusion

Theatre is implicated in the ethical struggles of the zones in which it exists. It does not sit above them. Every action performed, game played, question asked, story told and scene witnessed includes the theatre practitioner in an active ethical debate. Being implicated we must therefore start to carve out ways of understanding the limitations – the 'noes' and 'yeses' – of our work. While all values will be negotiated within the contexts that are encountered, we must not be afraid of starting to state what those values are. We need to confront that Kantian ghost so that values are openly presented and transformed in practice rather than simply being a spectre haunting our work. Although it may be fashionable within postmodernism to celebrate the 'demise of the ethical' (Bauman, 1993, p. 2), we should not use relativism as an excuse for avoiding creating positions from the specifics of practice. Ethics are not 'another illusion the postmodern men and women can well do without' (Bauman, 1993, p. 2) but a vital generator of the theatre we do in and with communities.

Theatre projects in war situations are part of that situation – part of the war – not separate from it. In pretending to an epistemic relation, we are guilty of denying our participation in the incidents that we study. As a participant, we need clarity in the values we bring even if we are confident that we will renegotiate them within the context. Although I agree with Daniel that the project of categorising and chronologising Sri Lanka's past is implicated in the divisions that caused the war, my worry about the artificial distance of epistemology has been tempered by the workshops I have conducted. Participants shifted continually from doing the workshops to learning to do the workshops. The Jaffna participants were in the work, and occasionally brought back by an insistence that they look again or in a different way. The Anuradhapura participants created their own rules to pull people away from real lived-in moments so that they could maintain their positions as learners, but also so that they could communicate on effect not cause. My belief that single narratives are implicated in violence (in the same way that the project of creating *a*

194

Sri Lankan history can be implicated in the divisions on the island) was challenged by the context of immediate war in Jaffna. Sometimes emphasising the single narrative can give sustenance to those experiencing a particular form of violence. Similarly, my belief in the power of both telling and listening to stories as a necessary precursor and constituent part of community dialogue was complicated by finding the situation in Anuradhapura, where silence, areas of taboo and lack of specificity enabled a group to communicate across differences.

Finally, the child soldiers project showed me that without explicit values our practice could become an easy target for appropriation and misrepresentation. However tenuously these values are held, and however willing one might be to re-evaluate them continually in light of experience, they should be honestly stated. If we do not say why we are doing our work, what our beliefs are and why we work with particular communities, someone else will do it for us. A transitive theatre is a break from a propagandist past practice in that it does not propose answers for others to accept. However, this does not mean it arrives empty handed. That desire to 'empower, enable, and give a voice' discussed at the beginning in the Strangeways project must be reconfigured, at least by recognising that we have a voice, a position, and a story to tell ourselves.

Every context has its own contested values and stories before we even meet a group of people living and working within it. They are often hard to grasp (to see) and only visible from certain directions or because of certain histories and experiences a person might have. Entering that situation with a (relativist) value vacuum will mean that other values will be attached to you, read in and through your actions whether you like it or not. Entering with a value position, however tentatively stated, will help to make those existing contextual values visible and potentially manageable. The child soldiers project and the problems with it – like all the Sri Lanka cases described here – became clearer the more strongly my position on the work was stated. This has of course happened as a result of my subsequent concerns, and was not articulated before the project was completed. For these reasons, I still think the practice was ethically questionable.

Two postscripts

On why the one ethical decision I made before going to Sri Lanka was wrong

The week before my first visit to Sri Lanka a women suicide bomber had blown herself up outside the Colombo town hall, killing a large number of people. My first value-inspired decision on visiting Sri Lanka was not to play the theatre game called 'Bombs and Shields' where participants have to chose a person in the group to be a human bomb and another to be their shield. An appropriate decision, I thought. Unfortunately, some of my Sri Lankan friends discovered I had made this decision without informing them and they insisted I play the game. I have played the game many times since. What can really be so troublesome about a theatre game?

Although I have to admit that the metaphor has been changed, during a visit in early 2001 I ran the game with a mixed Tamil/Sinhala group. In the game, wherever I run it, I do not say 'Choose a bomb', but instead 'Choose somebody in the room'. Only later do I tell them that this is a bomb. Similarly, I do not say 'Choose a shield', only 'Choose somebody', and later I say that this is now a shield. A Tamil colleague, actively involved in the struggle of the Tamil community in Sri Lanka for many years, found this exercise surprisingly moving. His comments on this game confounded the ethical simplicity of rejecting the exercise. 'Here I was,' he said, 'running away from a Sinhala man, but also hiding behind another Sinhala man'. Coincidentally, he had chosen a Sinhala person as his shield and was shocked by the physical effect of seeking shelter behind a member of a community from which he had normally felt threatened. This powerful moment would not have been possible if I had adhered to my original 'ethical' code.

In October 2000, while I was still writing the first notes for this chapter, several hundred people attacked the Bindunawewa re- habilitation camp where the theatre project had taken place. Out of roughly 80 detainees in the camp, 29 young men were killed and many more were injured. The dead were either burnt alive or killed with machetes. When I was there the youngest was 13 years old.

Each different group in the conflict has said what they think was happening at the camp. Major riots and demonstrations broke out in predominantly Tamil areas and there is a government inquiry into how it happened.

Implicated witness?
Participant observer?
Irresponsible responsible?
This is the place where it ends?

Ethically my shattered wings clink and clank with their knives.

Conclusion
Theatre garlands

A shadow world of petrified garlands (Gunesekera, 1994, p. 29)

Garlands are beautiful objects. They are heavy to hold and cold to wear. They thank, welcome, bid farewell, and honour. They speak of power, family, and community. They show submission and adulation. They are an occasion, a celebration, and a remembrance. However, they die, fade, and discolour quickly. They hang brightly for a moment, but beyond the ceremony, they are discarded. Simultaneously they are a wreath and a necklace. A flash of colour that announces, pronounces, and declares. They open and close. They are given from one to another. They are made, bought, sold, hung and thrown. They are extravagant, yet beautifully functional.

Garlanding – seeing them safely off or wrapping them safely in?

For a theatre of relief...?

Bland farces [...] provided some relief from the horrors of the time. (Harding, 1998, p. 12)

Do we want a theatre of relief, healing, reconciliation or liberation? Does applied theatre seek to wrap them in or see them safely off?

Applied theatre can be understood as a theatre practice with an explicit intent. It acts deliberately within institutions, with certain communities and on particular issues. It translates, adapts and transforms theatre processes so they work with, upon, between and against. The application has been characterised as a betwixt moment where neither the theatre nor the social environment or community group is stable. It is an unfinished act that generates its power within the process of the meeting of what are often highly different zones of practice. The application creates a friction that is the source of the energy or heat that forms the marks on and the bonds between people. Bewilderment is both the state of being confused within that moment of application, and the state of flux that can become the energetic creative force behind this use of theatre.

Much applied theatre in its 'intentional' form creates a practice that seeks to debate vital issues and see those concerns transformed into new stories or within unfamiliar settings. Applied theatre is populated with a great range of valuable drugs plays, AIDS education workshops, confidence-building processes and problem-solving drama games. However, while these are positive activities, I have suggested throughout this book that it is rarely in the transference of an explicit issue or skill that applied theatre finds its potential. The 'social energy' (Uphoff, 1996, pp. 357–87) derived from the process is a product of the clash of expectations, a change in intergroup relations and the meeting of the aesthetic with the mundane. The playing with fragments of action produces shifts within and between groups and communities. Participants perhaps reflect on aspects or concerns within their lives, but the action itself, in the live moment of the work, impacts in ways that are diverse, situation dependent and perhaps unconnected to the particular issue that the theatre project is focused upon. The heat of the theatre – project, performance or process – will carve, mould, mark or fuse according to the existing interconnections within the community and the patterns exhibited through the actions of participants. Provocatively, it could be argued that the issue is irrelevant. A theatre workshop on drugs education could involve one individual making a connection with an adult that they have not done before. It could include another stretching in a drama game to a place they have never reached. Or another laughing louder than they have ever done before in school. Yet another repeating a line from their mother in a scene of domestic tension or a child being amazed at their best friend's ability to perform personal grief. Clearly, this event cannot be narrowly analysed for the clarity of the understanding of drugs issues or the group's ability to say 'no' to temptation in small scenes of peer pressure.

Applied-theatre discussions must allow for clarity of intent, but at the same time not permit a denial of unpredictable and diverse effect. It is therefore not 'intentional' only in the sense that practitioners set clear aims and objectives for a particular applied-theatre programme. The intention is also revealed within the act of applying. The context and the participants provide further purpose and reason. The applied theatre this book has sought to advocate, therefore, is one that can have intent, but does not forget that this intent might have little to do with the actual event that it seeks to contain. This of course is echoed in all the arguments presented on ethics and practice principles. We cannot let dreams of a theatre with noble purpose batter the real uses of theatre in difficult and different spaces. At the same time, we must develop clarity as to what we believe that intention may be. So, while it may be easy to dismiss those 'bland farces' as having little value, in a time of 'horror' who is to say that relief is not a legitimate part of an applied theatre?

'Wrapping people in' might be the way that theatre works within a particular setting. A theatre of relief has value. It might act to protect, find coherence, bind and join individuals and communities at a time of extreme dislocation or bewilderment. Moments of major social or personal upheaval can therefore be eased, smoothed and secured by an engagement with forms of theatre that relieve, remind, warm and soothe. Singing, dancing, laughing and celebrating are thus an applied theatre in times of crisis because they provide a space of relief within the dangerous place of bewilderment. They are not the 'lowest form' (Harding, 1998, p. 13), but a valuable, vital means for sustaining people through difficult and perhaps horror-filled times. Theatre with displaced people, in prisons, with refugees, with excluded young people, too often assumes that the song and dance must be replaced with the serious scene. This makes a false division between the functional and the fun.

'Seeing them safely off' however is also a vital part of an applied-theatre practice. Bewilderment is a state that demands a protective response but also one that encourages people to move beyond troubling times and places. Much of the theatre discussed in this book has sought to provide people with a means to work their way through difficult transitory periods. Here the process offers an explanatory foothold and an experience that links a person into new networks – beyond the old. A damaged, hard-marked past can have fresh lines created through the experience of a participatory theatre project. These, as I have said repeatedly, might find new points of connection, allowing their potentially transformative quality to be reinforced in different moments. They do not guarantee any future behaviour. Although the reflection within the theatre process develops insights (footholds), these only become meaningful when they build and are given a direction by future experiences. The 'bridge across bewilderment' – for the many groups that engage in applied theatre – is created when the marks from the process 'intermesh within the wider context'. Applied theatre can be an aid in seeing them safely into a new place or time.

This book has also been a personal drive through the bewilderment of working with theatre in different places. The practice accounted for here has sought to move between the belief in the importance of lines in the sand and the need to disturb the easy frameworks within the moments of practice. It started with a proclamation of the importance of 'making a break', and how applied-theatre practice was more creative in times of 'bleary-eyed searching' than when it had a 'cognitive behavioural clarity'. However, in the process of writing the book new lines inevitably have been drawn. Principles have been alluded to, ways of seeing the work offered, critiques of practice suggested and ethics (almost) proposed. It has been necessary to attempt a move beyond that healthy bewilderment, to continue thinking and discussing this work. The final story, working with child soldiers in Sri Lanka, was the moment that the limit of relying on the creative impulse of 'not knowing' was reached. It was the top of the mountain, where finally principle should have been determinedly operative rather than negotiated. However flexible in the moment or responsive to the context, values and principles needed to impose themselves on this project without apology. They did not, and this was therefore a failing. Proposing theatre projects with difficult issues, excluded communities or vulnerable individuals must always have the line at the top of the mountain – while remembering that there is always perhaps, somewhere 'Just Over the Next Ridge'. The dance continues...

Skin-deep AT? Another palimpsest

Applied theatre, whether it be the transitive ideal from Boal ῾.
Freire, or the echo of a theatre for liberation from anti-Poll-Tax
cabarets, is constructed out of slivers, gestures, memories, actions and
marks in much the same way as the body as outlined in chapter one.
These lines bind it into other practices and mark it archeologically. It
is a palimpsest form that reveals multiple theatrical histories when its
surface is scratched, but also it is an emerging form that grows and is
re-marked in every new project.

This scratching and emerging are for me the current demands on
the field. There is much work to be done archaeologically examining
from where the practices that can be called applied theatre take their
influences, forms, and ideas. What are the histories, texts, rituals,
performance traditions, theories and politics that coalesce within
different practices of applied theatre? A scratching can reveal multiple
origins that will support our current understanding. However, applied
theatre also needs to build its knowledge base through an increase in
its practice. The 're-marking' must take place through practitioners,
communities, students and theatre companies continuing to develop
projects in existing and new settings. The balancing act between the
field that has an ethics but is sensitive to the negotiations demanded
by different contexts must continue to be danced.

Field, term or attitude?

There is always a danger in any field that claims it is 'emerging'.
Applied theatre is perhaps, more correctly, a *term* that is emerging
rather than a field. It covers practice which, as I say above, is rich in
its history and archaeology. As I say at the very beginning, it should
not aim to consume categories under a banner that could erase vital
differences in practice. I would claim that it is useful in supporting

connected practices, but it must also seek to coexist with a range of ways of understanding diverse theatre forms and approaches. Drama in education, theatre in education, theatre for development, community theatre and community-based performance (Haedicke and Nellhaus, 2001) do not disappear under its hungry umbrella. The rehearsal of the south Indian dance form Bharata Natyam in war-affected Sri Lanka could be applied theatre because it is a performance form used to provide a link for young Tamil people to their culture and give them relief from the conflict. It is wrapping them safely in. Using the term to describe this event allows comparisons to be made between different theatre projects within Sri Lanka that respond to the war, and in some ways permits similar comparisons to be made beyond the island. In addition, it contributes to debates on the relationship between function and form, traditional practice versus new, between the need to wrap them in or see them safely off. However, using 'applied theatre' in this case also runs the danger of simplifying differences and imposing categories that deny different histories. Bharata Natyam is of course also not applied theatre. The training in Sri Lanka is worthy of a considerably wider study that goes beyond simply asking how the dance applies itself to the needs of war-affected youth.

One of the primary reasons for concentrating here on projects with which I have either been directly involved or closely associated, is to avoid the ease with which categories can colonise different practices in programmes of aggrandisement. I am happy for applied theatre to be wielded in relation to projects close to me, but feel that it must be used more carefully when discussing events that do not use it as an organising term. My engagement with Atelier Théâtre Burkinabé is the story of an attempt to use my terms and frames of understanding without properly considering those that were constructed by the company already. Applied theatre is a powerful term with which to question, play and challenge a range of practice. However, it will always be an in-between category that is trying to find its place within types of theatre (whether it be Boalian or Bharata Natyam) and areas of social practice (whether it be prisoner rehabilitation or war relief). For this reason, we must use it to debate different practices in a diversity of settings, rather than frame it as a defining term for one unified approach.

Maybe it is therefore neither a field nor a term – but an attitude?

If it is an attitude, of course I commend it, share it, and would like to see it grow within the theatre-practitioner community and the diverse groups and places within which they work. The more theatre meets the challenges imposed by exclusion, discrimination, poverty and violence (wonderful value-filled words!), the happier I will become. The more we get on the ground and practice this difficult art form within the communities that have suffered bewilderment or with groups who have had their pasts marked with mistreatment, the more likely it is that an attitude will be able to call itself a 'field'. Multiple projects with an aptitude for making the engagement in theatre relevant and vital in the most unlikely of situations is a healthy aspiration – a positive attitude. This sounds worryingly like a call to action. If it is, it is time for me to get off the donkey, and start to feel the heat of the ground.

Bibliography

ANDERSON, J. (2000) *Second Year Report on ATB Forum Training Project* (London, Internal People's Palace Projects document)

ANISUR RAHMAN, M. D. (1993) *People's Self-Development: Perspectives on Participatory Action Research* (London, Zed Books)

ATB (1998a) *20ème Anniversaire* (leaflet, Ouagadougou, ATB)

—— (1998b) Festival Brochure (Ouagadougou, ATB)

—— (1998c) *Échos du Festival* (festival newspaper) (Ouagadougou, ATB)

AUSTIN, J. (1962) *How to Do Things with Words* (London, Oxford University Press)

BANDURA, A. (1977) *Social Learning Theory* (New Jersey, Prentice Hall)

BANHAM, M., J. Gibbs and F. Osofisan (eds) (1999) *African Theatre in Development* (Oxford, James Currey)

BAUMAN, Z. (1993) *Postmodern Ethics* (Oxford, Blackwell)

BHARUCHA, R. (1990) *Theatre and the World: Performance and the Politics of Culture* (London, Routledge)

—— (2000) *The Politics of Cultural Practice: Thinking Through Theatre in an Age of Globalisation* (London, Athlone Press)

BOAL, A. (1979) *Theatre of the Oppressed* (London, Pluto Press)

—— (1992) *Games for Actors and Non-Actors* (London, Routledge)

—— (1995) *Rainbow of Desire: The Boal Method of Theatre and Therapy* (London, Routledge)

—— (1998) *Legislative Theatre: Using Performance to Make Politics* (London, Routledge)

—— (2001) *Hamlet and the Baker's Son: My Life in Theatre and Politics* (London, Routledge)

BOON, R. and J. Plastow (eds) (1998) *Theatre Matters: Performance and Culture on the World Stage* (Cambridge, Cambridge University Press)

BYAM, L. D. (1998) 'Communal Space and Performance in Africa', in J. Cohen-Cruz (ed.) *Radical Street Performance: An International Anthology* (London, Routledge)

CAMPBELL, A., C. Matzke, G. Moriarty, R. O'Shea, J. Plastow and the Students of the Tigre/Bilen Theatre Training Course (1999) 'Telling the Lion's Tale: Making Theatre in Eritrea', in M. Banham, J. Gibbs and F.

Osofisan (eds) *African Theatre in Development* (Oxford, James Currey/Bloomington and Indianapolis, Indiana University Press)

CASE, S. E. and J. Reinelt (eds) (1991) *The Performance of Power: Theatrical Discourse and Politics* (Iowa City, University of Iowa Press)

CHAMBERS, R. (1997) *Whose Reality Counts? Putting the First Last* (London, Intermediate Technology Publications)

CHANDLER, M. J. (1973) 'Egocentrism and Antisocial Behaviour: the Assessment and Training of Social Perspective-Taking Skills', *Developmental Psychology*, 9.3, pp. 326–32

CHAPMAN, T. and M. Hough (1998) *Evidence Based Practice* (London, HMIP, HMSO)

CLIFFORD, J. and G. E. Marcus (eds) (1986) *Writing Culture: The Poetics and Politics of Ethnography* (Berkeley and London, University of California Press)

CLIFFORD, J. (1988) *The Predicament of Culture: Twentieth Century Ethnography, Literature and Art* (Cambridge (Mass.), Harvard University Press)

COHEN-CRUZ, J. (1998) (ed.) *Radical Street Performance: An International Anthology* (London, Routledge)

COHEN, L. and L. Manion (1994) *Research Methods in Education* (London, Routledge)

COX, M. (ed.) (1992) *Shakespeare Comes to Broadmoor: The Actors Come Hither* (London, Jessica Kingsley)

COLLERAN, J. and J. Spencer (eds) (1998) *Staging Resistance: Essays on Political Theater* (Ann Arbor, University of Michigan Press)

DANIEL, E. V. (1996) *Charred Lullabies: Chapters in an Anthropology of Violence* (Princeton, Princeton University Press)

DENNET, D. C. (1991) *Consciousness Explained* (London, Allen Lane)

DERRIDA, J. (1974) *Of Grammatology* (Baltimore, Johns Hopkins University Press)

—— (1978) *Writing and Difference* (Chicago, University of Chicago Press)

DE SILVA, K. M. (1998) *Reaping the Whirlwind: Ethnic Conflict, Ethnic Politics in Sri Lanka* (London, Penguin)

DIAMOND, E. (ed.) (1996) *Performance and Cultural Politics* (London, Routledge)

DUHAMEL, M. and V. Bordet (1994) *Étude d'une Practique du Théâtre Forum et de son Impact Socio-culturel: Mémoire de Maîtrise* (Paris, Université de Paris III – Sorbonne Nouvelle)

EDMISTON, B. (2000) 'Drama as Ethical Education', *Research in Drama Education*, 5.1, pp. 63–84

FANON, F. (1986) *Black Skin, White Masks* (London, Pluto Press)

FINN, M. (2001) 'Celibates in Ivory Tower Find Stardom', *Times Higher Education Supplement*, 9 November 2001, pp.16–17

FREIRE, P. (1970) *Pedagogy of the Oppressed* (London, Penguin)

FOUCAULT, M. (1977) *Discipline and Punish: The Birth of the Prison* (London, Allen Lane)

GAINOR, J. E. (1995) *Imperialism and Theatre: Essays on World Theatre, Drama and Performance* (London, Routledge)

GARLAND, D. (1990) *Punishment and Society: A Study in Social Theory* (Oxford University Press)

GEERTZ, C. (1973) *The Interpretation of Cultures* (London, Fontana Press)

GENDREAU, P. (1996) 'The Principles of Effective Intervention with Offenders', in A. T. Harland (ed.) *Choosing Correctional Options that Work* (London, Sage)

Getting Our Act Together: *A Manual for the Delivery of Key Skills and Basic Skills through Drama* (2002, Canterbury)

GOLDSTEIN, A. and B. Glick (1994) *The Pro-Social Gang: Implementing Aggression Replacement Training* (Thousand Oaks, California, Sage Publications)

GOYDER, H., R. Davies and W. Williamson (1998) *Participatory Impact Assessment* (London, Action Aid)

GRADY, S. (1996) 'Towards the Practice of Theory in Practice', in P. Taylor (ed.) *Researching Drama and Arts Education: Paradigms and Possibilities* (London, Falmer Press)

GREENWOOD, D. J. and M. Levin (1998) *Introduction to Action Research: Social Research for Social Change* (London, Sage Publications)

GUNARATNA, R. (1998) *Sri Lanka's Ethnic Crisis and National Security* (Colombo, South Asian Network on Conflict Research)

GUNSEKERA, R. (1994) *Reef* (London, Granta Books)

HAEDICKE, S. C. and T. Nellhaus (eds) (2001) *Performing Democracy: International Perspectives on Urban Community-based Performance* (Ann Arbor, University of Michigan Press)

HARDING, F. (1998) *'Neither "Fixed Masterpiece" nor "Popular Distraction": Voice, Transformation and Encounter in Theatre for Development'*, in K. Sahli (ed.) *African Theatre for Development Art for Self-Determination* (Exeter, Intellect)

HARLAND, A. T. (ed.) (1996) *Choosing Correctional Options that Work* (London, Sage Publications)

HERITAGE, P. (1998a) 'Theatre, Prisons and Citizenship: A South American Way', in J. Thompson (ed.) *Prison Theatre: Perspectives and Practices* (London, Jessica Kingsley Publishers)

—— (1998b) 'The Promise of Performance: True Love/Real Love', in R. Boon and J. Plastow (eds) *Theatre Matters: Performance and Culture on the World Stage* (Cambridge, Cambridge University Press)

HOLLIN, C. R. (1990) *Cognitive-Behavioural Interventions with Young Offenders* (New York, Pergamon Press)

HOME OFFICE (1991) *Custody, Care and Justice: the Way Ahead for the Prison Service in England and Wales*, Cm 1647 (London, HMSO)

HORTON, M. and P. Freire (1990) *We Make the Road by Walking: Conversations on Education and Social Change* (Philadelphia, Temple University Press)

JEYIFO, B. (1996) *The Reinvention of Theatrical Tradition: Critical Discourses in the African Theatre*, in P. Pavis (ed.) *The Intercultural Performance Reader* (London, Routledge)

KEMMIS, S. and R. McTaggart (1988) *The Action Research Planner* (Geelong, Victoria Deakin University Press)

KERR, D. (1999) 'Art as Tool, Weapon or Shield? Arts for Development Seminar, Harare', in M. Banham, J. Gibbs and F. Osofisan (eds) *African Theatre in Development* (Oxford, James Currey)

KERSHAW, B. (1999) *The Radical in Performance: Between Brecht and Baudrillard* (London, Routledge)

KING, R. D. and R. Morgan (1980) *The Future of the Prison System* (Farnborough, Gower)

LANDY, R. J. (1993) *Persona and Performance: The Meaning of Role in Drama, Therapy and Everyday Life* (London, Jessica Kingsley)

LATERAL ASSOCIATES (1999) 'The Greater Manchester Employment Project at Buckley Hall' (Manchester, internal document)

LAZARUS, N. (1999) *Nationalism and Cultural Practice in the Postcolonial World* (Cambridge, Cambridge University Press)

'L'Étude d'impact du Théâtre-Forum sur le developpement' (1998) (Ouagadougou, Société Africaine d'Étude et Conseils, unpublished report)

LEWIN, K. (1946) 'Action Research and Minority Problems', *Journal of Social Issues*, 2 (1946), pp. 34–46

MARTINSON, R. (1974) 'What Works?' – Questions and Answers about Prison Reform', *The Public Interest*, 35 (1974), pp. 22–54

MCGUIRE, J. (ed.) (1995) What Works: *Reducing Reoffending* (London, Wiley and Sons)

MCNIFF, J. (1988) *Action Research: Principles and Practice* (London, Routledge)

MOONEERAM, R. (1999) 'Theatre for Development in Mauritius: From Theatre of Protest to a Theatre of Cultural Miscegenation', in M. Banham, M. J. Gibbs and F. Osofisan (eds) *African Theatre in Development* (Oxford, James Currey)

MORRISON, J. (1991) Communication and Social Change: A Case Study of Forum Theater in Burkina Faso (unpublished thesis for Doctor of Philosophy Degree in Mass Communications in Graduate College of the University of Iowa)

MUNCK, R. and D. O'Hearn (1999) *Critical Development Theory: Contributions to a New Paradigm* (London, Zed books)

NARAYAN SWAMY, M. R. (1994) *Tigers of Lanka: From Boys to Guerrillas* (Colombo, Vijitha Yapa)

OBEYESEKERE, R. (1999) *Sri Lankan Theater in a Time of Terror: Political Satire in a Permitted Space* (New Delhi, Sage Publications)

OKAGBU, O. (1998) 'Product or Process: Theatre for Development in Africa', in K. Sahli (ed.) *African Theatre for Development: Art for Self-Determination* (Exeter, Intellect)

PARKER, I. (ed.) (1998) *Social Constructionism, Discourse and Realism* (London, Sage Publications)

PAVIS, P. (1992) *Theatre at the Crossroads of Culture* (London, Routledge)

—— (ed) (1996) *The Intercultural Performance Reader* (London, Routledge)

PHELAN, P. (1993a) *Unmarked: The Politics of Performance* (London, Routledge)

—— (1993b) 'Reciting the Citation of Others; Or, A Second Introduction', in L. Hart and P. Phelan (eds) *Acting Out: Feminist Performances* (Michigan, University of Michigan Press)

PLASTOW, J. (1998) 'Uses and Abuses of Theatre for Development: Political Struggle and Development Theatre in the Ethiopia–Eritrea War', in K. Sahli (ed.) *African Theatre for Development: Art for Self-Determination* (Exeter, Intellect)

POOLE, L. (1996) *Evaluation of the Clever Project: A Drama Project in Hindley Young Offender Institution* (Manchester, Practice Development Unit, Greater Manchester Probation Service)

POTTER, J. and M. Wetherell (1987) *Discourse and Social Psychology: Beyond Attitudes and Behaviour* (London, Sage Publications)

POTTER, J. (1996) *Representing Reality: Discourse, Rhetoric and Social Construction* (London, Sage Publications)

211

PRIESTLEY, P. and J. McGuire (1985) *Offending Behaviour: Skills and Stratagems for Going Straight* (London, Batsford)

RABINOW, P. (1986) 'Representations are Social Facts: Modernity and Post-Modernity in Anthropology', in J. Clifford and G. E. Marcus (eds) *Writing Culture: The Poetics and Politics of Ethnography* (Berkeley and London, University of California Press)

REINELT, J. and J. Roach (eds) (1992) *Critical Theory and Performance* (Ann Arbor, University of Michigan Press)

REINELT, J. (ed.) (1996) *Crucibles of Crisis: Performing Social Change* (Ann Arbor, University of Michigan Press)

ROACH, J. (1996) 'Kinship, Intelligence, and Memory as Improvisation: Culture and Performance in New Orleans', in E. Diamond (ed.) *Performance and Cultural Politics* (London, Routledge)

ROSE, S. (1998) *Group Therapy with Troubled Youth: A Cognitive-Behavioural Interactive Approach* (London, Sage)

ROSENBERG, M. (1965) *Society and the Adolescent Self-image* (Princeton, Princeton University Press)

ROTBERG, R. (ed.) (1999) *Creating Peace in Sri Lanka: Civil War and Reconciliation* (Washington, DC, Brookings Institution Press)

SAHLI, K. (ed) (1998) *African Theatre for Development: Art for Self-Determination* (Exeter, Intellect)

SALDAÑA, J. (1998) 'Ethical Issues in an Ethnographic Performance Text: The "Dramatic Impact" of "Juicy Stuff"', *Research in Drama Education,* 3. 2 (1998), pp.181–96

SALOMAN, G. (1993) *Distributed Cognition* (Cambridge, Cambridge University Press)

SCHECHNER, R. (1988) *Performance Theory* (London, Routledge)

—— (1993) *The Future of Ritual* (London, Routledge)

—— (2002) *Performance Studies: An Introduction* (London, Routledge)

SCHEURICH, J. J. (1997) *Research Method in the Postmodern* (Falmer Press, London)

SCHONMANN, S. (1996) 'Jewish–Arab Encounters in the Drama/Theatre Class Battlefield', *Research in Drama Education,* 1.2 (1996), pp.175–187

SHELDON, B. (1995) *Cognitive Behavioural Therapy: Research, Practice and Philosophy* (London, Routledge)

SHUTTLEWORTH, T. (1994) *Lancaster Farms – 'Acting out – inside' Drama Project Evaluation Report* (Manchester, Practice Development Unit, Greater Manchester Probation Service)

212

SIMON, F. (1999) *Prisoner's Work and Vocational Training* (London, Routledge)

SPAAS, L. (2000) *The Francophone Film: A Struggle for Identity* (Manchester, Manchester University Press)

STONE PETERS, J. (1995) 'Intercultural Performance, Theatre Anthropology, and the Imperialist Critique: Identities, Inheritances, and Neo-Orthodoxies', in J. E. Gainor (ed.) *Imperialism and Theatre: Essays on World Theatre, Drama and Performance* (London, Routledge)

TAYLOR, P. (ed.) (1996) *Researching Drama and Arts Education: Paradigms and Possibilities* (London, Falmer Press)

THOMPSON, J. (1995) 'Blagg! Rehearsing for Change', *Probation Journal*, 42 (1995), pp.190–94

—— (ed.) (1998) *Prison Theatre: Perspectives and Practices* (London, Jessica Kingsley)

—— (1999a) *Drama Workshops for Anger Management and Offending Behaviour* (London, Jessica Kingsley)

—— (1999b) '"Nous sommes, vous êtes comédiens…" Celebrating Twenty Years of Theatre for Development in Burkina Faso', *Research in Drama Education*, 4.1 (1999), pp.107–11

—— (2001) 'Making a Break for It: Discourse and Theatre in Prisons', *Applied Theatre Researcher*, 2 (www.gu.edu.au/text/centre/atr/opt6/frameset1b2.html)

—— (2002) 'Motivating Offenders to Change through Theatre', in McMurran, M. (ed.) *Motivating Offenders to Change* (London, Wiley and Sons)

TURNER, V. (1982) *From Ritual to Theatre: The Human Seriousness of Play* (New York, Performing Arts Journal Publications)

—— (1987) *The Anthropology of Performance* (New York, Performing Arts Journal Publications)

TYLER, S. (1986) 'Post-Modern Ethnography: From Document of the Occult to Occult Document', in J. Clifford and G. E. Marcus (eds) *Writing Culture: The Poetics and Politics of Ethnography* (Berkeley and London, University of California Press)

UPHOFF, N. (1996) *Learning from Gal Oya: Possibilities for a Post-Newtonian Social Science* (London, Intermediate Technology Publications)

WILSON, A. J. (2000) *Sri Lankan Tamil Nationalism: Its Origins and Development in the 19th and 20th Centuries* (London, Hurst and Company)

WOOLF, H. and S. Tumin (1991) *Prison Disturbances April 1990: Report of an Inquiry*, Cm 1456 (London, HMSO)

ZARRILLI, P. (1992) 'For Whom is the King a King? Issues of Intercultural Production, Perception, and Reception in a Kathakali *King Lear*', in J. Reinelt and J. Roach (eds) *Critical Theory and Performance* (Ann Arbor, University of Michigan Press)

ZUBER-SKERRITT, O. (ed.) (1996) *New Directions in Action Research* (London, Falmer Press)

Index

217

219

S T S S
STAGE and SCREEN STUDIES

This series of monographs is concerned with drama and allied entertainment in a wide variety of kinds in the theatre and on film, television and video screens. The emphasis is on the history and interpretation of dramatic entertainment, performance and production in regular and musical theatre, including music hall and variety stages, in para-theatrical activities, like fairground performance and festivals, and in the silent and sound cinema and on television and video.

The series engages particularly with the social, political and economic contexts of drama on past and present stages and screens, considering the work of dramatists, performers, directors, designers, technicians and administrators, and will aim to be very wide-ranging in scope, its subjects spanning Classical, Medieval and Renaissance European drama and theatre, Eastern theatre forms, and international modern drama in its various performance kinds. Within this broad remit, the series hopes to publish historical, critical and theoretical studies, annotated anthologies of critical, theoretical and dramatic texts, and collections of interviews and screenplays.

Vol. 4   Stephen Chinna
          Performance: Recasting the Political in Theatre and Beyond
          220 pp. 2003.
          ISBN 3-03910-000-9 / US-ISBN 0-8204-5921-6

Vol. 5   James Thompson
          Applied Theatre: Bewilderment and Beyond
          220 pp. 2003.
          ISBN 3-03910-021-1 / US-ISBN 0-8204-6290-X

Malgorzata Bartula / Stefan Schroer

On Improvisation

Nine Conversations with Roberto Ciulli

Bruxelles, Bern, Berlin, Frankfurt/M., New York, Oxford, Wien, 2003.
164 pp., num. ill.
Dramaturgies. Texts, Cultures and Performances. Vol. 12
General Editor: Marc Maufort
ISBN 90-5201-185-0 / US-ISBN 0-8204-6604-2 pb.
sFr. 27.– / €1* 18.10 / €2** 16.90 / £ 11.– / US-$ 16.95

* *The €1-price includes VAT and is only valid for Germany and Austria.*
** *The €2-price does not include VAT.*

Roberto Ciulli is one of the most exciting and provocative theatre directors of our time. In these conversations he expounds the transformative ideas on theatrical improvisation which have challenged actors and audiences alike to rethink what they understand the nature of theatre practice to be. Using examples from more than twenty years of innovative performances with the Theater an der Ruhr, he describes the workshop process, the long-term personal commitment, and the political and aesthetic concepts driving his view of theatre as an agent of social change. His pioneering espousal of internationalisation as a basic principle of contemporary theatre work has won him great acclaim, particularly for his intercultural «Silk Road Project» with theatre companies in Central Asia.

These conversations have been translated by Geoffrey Davis, who teaches at the University of Aachen.

Contents: First Conversation: Freedom in Prison – Second Conversation: The Age of Apes – Third Conversation: A Better Prison – Fourth Conversation: Life Is the Most Difficult Art – Fifth Conversation: Life Belongs to the Actor – Sixth Conversation: Working on the Creation of Something New in the Green Fields – Seventh Conversation: Theatre for the Outsider – Eighth Conversation: Myself as a Member of the Audience – Ninth Conversation: A Global Effect – Helmut Schäfer - Invitation to the Dream – Roberto Ciulli - Biographical Data – The Theater an der Ruhr.

PETER LANG
Bern · Berlin · Bruxelles · Frankfurt/M. · New York · Oxford · Wien

Stephen Chinna
Performance
Recasting the Political in Theatre and Beyond

Oxford, Bern, Berlin, Bruxelles, Frankfurt/M., New York, Wien, 2003. 220 pp.
Stage and Screen Studies. Vol. 4
Edited by Kenneth Richards
ISBN 3-03910-000-9 / US-ISBN 0-8204-5921-6 pb.
sFr. 67.– / €1* 46.10 / €2** 43.10 / £ 28.– / US-$ 42.95

* *The €1-price includes VAT and is only valid for Germany and Austria.*
** *The €2-price does not include VAT.*

This book is an analysis and study of postmodernism, political theatre, and the politics of representation. Traversing a wide span of twentieth-century political theatre and performance practices in the West, the author analyses and questions the performance practices of the historical and neo-avant-gardes, modernist political theatre, and postmodern performance in order to explore the relationships between politics, performance and post-modernism. Chinna contends that it is the provisional and contingent strategies of performance which set the model for the postmodern. Drawing on the poststructuralist theories of Jean-Francois Lyotard and Jacques Derrida, among others, the postmodern is defined as a performance model – like deconstruction, endlessly deferring unequivocal meaning and final closure. It is argued that historical avant-garde performance practices such as Dada, as well as the neo-avant-gardes from the 1950s onward, were always trapped within a dialectic of representation and the 'real' in their quest for a merging of art and life.

Contents: Postmodernism – Postmodern political strategies – Postmodern Performance – Deconstruction – The Politics of Representation – Historical and Neo-avant-garde Theatre Practices – Modernism – Political Theatre.

PETER LANG
Bern · Berlin · Bruxelles · Frankfurt/M. · New York · Oxford · Wien